General editor: Graham Handley MA

Brodie's Notes on J. D. Salinger's

The Catcher in the Rye

Catherine Madinaveitia BA (Hons.) PG Cert. Ed.
English Department, Watford Grammar School for Girls

Pan Books London, Sydney and Auckland

First published 1987 by Pan Books Ltd,
Cavaye Place, London SW10 9PG
9 8 7 6 5 4 3
© Pan Books Ltd 1987
ISBN 0 330 50255 7
Photoset by Parker Typesetting Service, Leicester
Printed and bound in Great Britain by
Richard Clay Ltd, Bungay, Suffolk

Contents

Page references in these Notes are to the Penguin paperback edition of J. D. Salinger's *The Catcher in the Rye* but as references are also made to individual chapters, the Notes may be used with any edition of the novel.

Preface

The intention throughout this study aid is to stimulate and guide, to encourage the reader's *involvement* in the text, to develop disciplined critical responses and a sure understanding of the main details.

Brodie's Notes provide a summary of the plot of the play or novel followed by act, scene or chapter summaries, each of which will have an accompanying critical commentary designed to emphasize the most important literary and factual details. Poems, stories or non-fiction texts will combine brief summary with critical commentary on either individual aspects or sequences of the genre being considered. Textual notes will be explanatory or critical (sometimes both), defining what is difficult or obscure on the one hand, or stressing points of character, style, plot or the technical aspects of poetry on the other. Revision questions will be set at appropriate points to test the student's careful application to the text of the prescribed book.

The second section of each of these study aids will consist of a critical examination of the author's art. This will cover such major elements as characterization, style, structure, setting, theme(s) for example in novels, plays or stories; in poetry it will deal with the types of poem, rhyme, rhythm, free verse for example, or in non-fiction with the main literary concerns of the work. The editor may choose to examine any aspect of the book being studied which he or she considers to be important. The paramount aim is to send the student back to the text. Each study aid will include a series of general questions which require detailed knowledge of the set book: the first of these questions will have notes by the editor of what *might* be included in a written answer. A short list of books considered useful as background reading for the student will be provided at the end.

The General Certificate of Secondary Education in Literature

These study aids are suitable for candidates taking the new GCSE examinations in English Literature since they provide detailed preparation for examinations in that subject as well as presenting critical ideas and commentary of major use to candidates preparing their coursework files. These aids provide a basic, individual and imaginative response to the appreciation of literature. They stimulate disciplined habits of reading, and they will assist the responsive student to analyse and to write about the texts with discrimination and insight.

Graham Handley

Literary terms used in these Notes

Ambiguous (Chapter 24) Capable of several interpretations, as when Mr Antolini strokes Holden's hair in the night.

Anticlimax (Chapter 6) Emotion is built up to a peak then suddenly let down. Holden attacks Stradlater in fury but is beaten off easily.

Bathos (Chapter 7) A sudden shift from the sublime to the trivial which usually produces humour; for example, when Holden spoils his exit from Pencey by falling on the stairs.

Burlesque (Chapter 8) An imitation of serious ideas with the intention of making fun of them. Holden's outrageous conversation with Mrs Morrow about Ernest is wildly improbable and therefore highly amusing.

Black comedy (Chapter 12) Human suffering made to appear comic because it is conveyed without compassion. Holden's use of the cinema technique to diminish his suffering and his misunderstandings with Horwitz are black comedy.

Cliché (Chapters 2,3 and 9) A phrase or idea that has been used so much that it has ceased to be meaningful. Holden speaks largely in clichés; even his swearing is clichéd.

Digressions (Chapter 24) Anecdotes inserted at seemingly random points in the narrative which veer from the point under discussion. They occur throughout the book.

Dramatic irony (Structure Note 4) The reader being aware of a hidden significance that the characters do not know. For example, the reader is asked to notice Holden's own immaturity when he discusses his dislike of Al Pike – the result of his own unacknowledged jealousy.

Euphemism Using a gentle phrase to disguise something unpalatable or crude. For example, the reference made by Marty from Seattle to the toilet in Chapter 10. (See also section on *Style*.)

Imagery (Chapter 22) Comparisons between two or more unrelated ideas which extend the reader's understanding. For example, the concept of the Catcher standing in the ryefield gives a vivid picture of Holden's mental state.

Irony (Chapters 4 and 7) A mild form of sarcasm causing humour because of the effect of the unfairness expressed. For example, it was ironic that Holden should be asked to write an essay because he had been expelled for inattention.

Picaresque (Structure Note 1) A type of novel written in the first person, using colloquial language which explores society through a series of adventures. *The Catcher in the Rye* is a picaresque novel.

Stream of consciousness (Chapter 18) A technique of writing in which ideas and thoughts are noted down seemingly at random, without form or rearrangement. *The Catcher in the Rye* uses this to a certain extent.

Symbol (Style Note 3) A simple image or idea which represents much more, like the record, the carousel or Jane Gallagher.

Theme (Chapter 2) An idea or prevailing motif.

Understatement (Chapter 3) Saying less than is meant for the sake of effect.

The life and work of J. D. Salinger

Jerome David Salinger was born in New York on 1 January 1919. He was the second child and only son of an Irish mother, Marie, now Miriam, Jillich and Sol Salinger, a well-to-do Jewish importer.

He has been described as a normal, quiet boy, who enjoyed the usual pursuits; reading, acting and walking, tennis, and pool. He was not outstanding academically, dropped out of Manhattan's McBurney School and went to a military school, Valley Forge Academy, where some of the material for *The Catcher in the Rye* originated. In 1937 he spent some time in Europe. He attended three colleges, but left without qualifications.

His first publication was *The Young Folks*, in March 1940, arising from a course he took at Columbia University. After that, other stories were published in various magazines, starting with the *Saturday Evening Post* and *Colliers* (1941–5).

During this time he was drafted into the army. He did clerical work and wrote publicity releases. In 1943 he joined the Intelligence Corps of the 4th Infantry Division as a Staff Sergeant and was shipped overseas for two and a half years. He spent a brief period of training in Devon and stayed in the Army through five campaigns from D-Day (June 1944) to the end of the war, when he was married briefly to a doctor. Later he returned to his parents' home in New York. There he enjoyed a full social life, until he became interested in Zen Buddhism, and began to go away on periodic retreats to write.

In 1953 when he was 34 he met his future wife Claire Douglas, then a student at Radcliffe. When she married someone else, he erected a barrier around his house and became a recluse. Later, in 1955, Claire Douglas divorced her first husband and married Salinger but he continued to lead the life of a recluse. He resents intrusion, refuses to comment on his work and will not give interviews. In 1961 *Time* magazine published an article about him; the now famous cover photograph simply showed a drawing of Salinger as the author had refused to allow a photograph of himself to be used.

In 1951 *The Catcher in the Rye* was published. It was immediately associated with the contemporary literary expressions of rebellion against society, such as *Look Back in Anger* by John Osborne. In its time and for a decade afterwards it aroused controversy. It has been banned in various countries: in San Jose (USA) in Australia (1957) and in South Africa (1958). Teachers in America have been suspended for issuing the book to pupils, because of the degree of obscenity and in particular the one four-letter word which, incidentally, also disgusted Holden. On the other hand it has been praised for its accurate portrayal of the speech of the American teenager of the 'Fifties, and its sentiments still find a sympathetic echo worldwide.

In 1953, a selection of Salinger's stories appeared, called *For Esmé- with love and squalor* or *Nine Short Stories*. The title story tells of an American soldier stationed in Britain who meets an English girl, and of the watch she sends him as a talisman which restores his faith in life. This however is the most optimistic of the stories. The others detail disillusionment, and the inevitability of misery. 'A Perfect Day for Bananafish', for example, contains a delightful episode with a man entertaining a little girl on a beach, and ends abruptly with his suicide only moments later. In 1955 a short novel, *Franny* was published, to be re-issued with a companion novelette, *Zooey* in 1961. These two take up the motif that Salinger started on in some of his *Nine Stories*, the saga of the Glass Family. The Glasses were a husband and wife vaudeville act, who had seven children. The stories about them are odd, and ultimately depressing because they conclude without positive change. *Franny* and *Raise High the Roofbeam, Carpenters* (1963) deal with the incompatability of two couples. *Seymour, an Introduction* published in 1959, tries to explain some of the reasons for the suicide described in 'A Perfect Day for Bananafish'. Salinger has published nothing since.

Plot summary

The narrator, Holden Caulfield, is about to recount the experiences he had at the end of the autumn term a year before, when he was sixteen. Various biographical details emerge, in spite of his explicit refusal to give us any. His parents are private, reticent people who might be angry if he were to gossip about them. He briefly refers to visits from his older brother, DB, and boasts of his Jaguar car and writing talent. Although Holden is not specific, he seems to be writing from somewhere near Hollywood where he has gone to rest.

Holden's story starts on a windy December day, after his return from a trip with the fencing team to New York. He has just been expelled from Pencey, his expensive private boarding-school, for failing four of his five subjects. He has already been expelled from two other schools for the same reason. He hurries to pay a farewell visit to his old history teacher who is ill.

Mr Spencer is fond of Holden and tries to make him understand that he should pay more attention to his work, but Holden, although outwardly polite, refuses to listen. He is very concerned about the phoney people he meets; in his opinion there is nothing worse than phoniness. On his return to his room, Holden is visited by a fellow student whom he regards as a bore. Holden's room-mate Stradlater arrives and asks Holden to write an essay for him because he has a date. When Holden learns that Stradlater's date is an old friend of his, he begins to feel jealous and depressed. He refuses to go downstairs to see her.

Later that evening, Holden writes the essay on the subject of his dead brother Allie's baseball mitt. We are told that Allie died of leukaemia three years before. Holden remembers him with great affection, and treasures his mitt, on which Allie wrote scraps of poetry. When Stradlater returns and comments disparagingly on the subject-matter of the essay, Holden tears it up. He is now so obsessed with fears about Stradlater's date with Jane, whose virginity has taken on a symbolic importance, that he starts a fight with him which he inevitably loses. After failing to get sympathy and comfort from another student, Holden impulsively leaves Pencey three days early.

He takes the train to New York, and goes to a shabby hotel because he does not want to be at home when his parents receive the headmaster's letter of expulsion. He is now alone in the adult world, and meets a variety of characters, all of whom are either sleazy or phoney in some way. He visits two nightclubs that evening, and is offered a prostitute by the pimp of a lift-boy. Although he instantly regrets doing so, he accepts, and is then too depressed and self-conscious to have sex when she arrives. She later returns with the pimp who beats him up and takes money from his wallet.

The next morning Holden telephones his girlfriend, and arranges to take her to a matinée. Later, he overhears a little boy singing a song which Holden mistakenly believes to be 'If a body catch a body coming through the rye'. He is very impressed by the child's happiness, and the idea of the song stays in his mind. He buys a record for his young sister Phoebe and hastens away from the dismal cinema queues to the park where he hopes to find her. He walks over to the museum, but she isn't there.

Holden's date with his girlfriend Sally is a failure. He finds the spectators even more phoney than the actors. Sally has a gushing reunion with an acquaintance, which annoys Holden. Afterwards at the skating rink, he asks Sally to elope with him and live in a cabin in the wilds. Sally refuses, and they argue. Holden then arranges to meet Carl Luce, a schoolfriend who is three years his senior and whose opinions he respects. He is anxious to ask him about sexual relationships, but Luce sneers pretentiously at him, remarks on his lack of maturity, and leaves him alone in the bar, where Holden proceeds to get drunk.

Holden becomes morbidly depressed, making his way to the park where he unintentionally breaks the record he bought for Phoebe. He thinks of his dead brother Allie, and throws away all the money he has left. The thought of his sister revives him from his melancholy. He decides to visit her, and creeps into her room while his parents are out. His parents return and he goes to spend the night at the home of Mr Antolini, one of his ex-teachers. Mr Antolini, like Mr Spencer, tries to communicate with Holden. During the night Holden awakes to find Mr Antolini sitting by his bed, caressing his head. Holden is terrified of homosexuality, and leaves immediately. He spends a miserable night in the station, and the next morning decides to make his way out West to his dreamed-of cabin. He meets Phoebe, who has already packed her case, and insists on going with him. After a quarrel, Holden agrees to go home with her. The novel ends as he stands watching her on the roundabout, drenched in the rain, happy at last as he feels needed and loved.

Chapter commentaries, textual notes and revision questions

Chapter 1

The direct, conversational style of the narrator makes an immediate impact on the reader. Holden Caulfield speaks as though he knows us throughout the novel; he expects us to take an active part in his life. He includes us in his judgements and decisions, and because of this participation, the reader feels a sympathy for him and an affinity with his attitudes which carries us with him through the book.

Although Holden's idioms are not all familiar, the tone is very much that of a teenage American boy of the fifties. The novel has been praised for its colloquial quality: Holden speaks in a vivid, gritty and immediate style. There is some coarseness in the epithets he uses, and indeed when the book was first taught in American schools there were protests against some of the language.

Holden's sentences are loosely strung together and sometimes he veers off to another subject. This style of speech is conversational and true to life and the same can be said of his expressions. He is fond of adding 'and all' as if unsure how to end a sentence and he is also given to inventing words. Another of Holden's idiosyncrasies is to question the reader as to whether he really wants to know what he has to say – a sign of his insecurity. Further evidence of this insecurity can be seen in his qualifying much of what he says.

Holden's views on several subjects are surprisingly different from those of his contemporaries. He is honest in his assessments, not at all blinded by social pressures. In fact even at the beginning of the story he comes over as a loner. He feels no sense of loyalty to his school, nor is he impressed by its character-building aims so stressed in the advertisements. He refers contemptuously to the Headmaster. He is not interested in the football game which engrosses the rest of the boys. There are various reasons which could account for his independence of mind. He feels alienated from the other pupils. He has been expelled by the Headmaster, and ostracized by the fencing team. He has already been asked to leave other schools and his life has continued much as before so he feels no dread of the future. He does not blame himself for his lack of progress.

There are events in his life over which he feels he has no control, and which he casually accepts, like the theft of his expensive camel's hair coat and fur-lined gloves. Money has been lavished on him. Apart from bemoaning how cold he feels, he seems to blame the environment of the school for the existence of crooks.

Holden is emotional in his responses. He does not want to leave Pencey without a feeling of farewell; he dreads an emotional vacuum. He runs impulsively across the road to Mr Spencer's house, and feels a sensation of exhilaration. He also makes a remark which is echoed and magnified at the end of the book – that he feels as though he is 'disappearing' when he crosses the road.

The chapter ends on a note of impatience intensified by the extreme cold; he is so eager for the door to open that he practically speaks to it.

David Copperfield kind of crap *David Copperfield* (1849–50) is a largely autobiographical novel by Charles Dickens in which the narrator tells the story of his life in minute detail beginning, 'I am born. . .' Evidently Holden does not appreciate the style.

have about two haemorrhages apiece One of Holden's characteristic overstatements. He means here that his parents would be furious.

just a regular writer An ordinary writer.

being a prostitute Used metaphorically in this case. Holden means that his brother is not making full use of his talent, selling inferior work for money.

hot-shot guy (slang) An athletic, self-confident young man.

strictly for the birds (slang) Not to be believed.

Old Pencey, old Selma Thurmer The epithet 'old' indicates Holden's feeling of affection tinged with contempt. This is one of Holden's running clichés, not associated with age.

way the hell up on top Needless insertion of 'the hell' adds emphasis.

crazy cannon Crazy applied to cannon indicates an amazement that it should exist at all, let alone be up on top of the hill.

falsies (slang) A type of padded brassiere popular in the fifties.

fencing meet A fencing match.

grippe Influenza, 'flu.

the axe (slang) Expulsion.

cold as a witch's teat A vulgar simile for expressing the freezing temperature.

reversible A lined coat, specially made so it can be worn either way out.

Mr Zambesi The Zambesi is a river in Africa; perhaps the teacher was black.

Chapter 2

This chapter describes the attempt of Mr Spencer to communicate with Holden. Spencer's speech is pedantic; he uses long words, calls Holden 'boy' instead of using his name, and speaks in clichés. Holden's gradual loss of sympathy and growing embarrassment with Mr Spencer as the interview proceeds are expressed in the more frequent use of asides and irrelevancies as his mind seeks more congenial images.

The reader should bear in mind that Holden often exaggerates, reacting naively to appearances. For instance, it is unlikely that Mr Spencer would really be over 70, and it is improbable that he was physically unable to pick up chalk from the floor. Mr Spencer in fact takes an interest in his pupils, inviting them to share in his private life. Holden says he was one of a group of boys over there at the weekend; Mrs Spencer doesn't have to treat him like a guest, and he thinks she likes him. Mr Spencer tries to make Holden understand that he is jeopardizing his future by his indifference, but this is something Holden is blind to. Although Mr Spencer is one of the few adults that Holden respects, he is much antagonized by this attempt to make him face reality.

Holden manages to combine unexpected, honest appreciation with obtuse insensitivity. He recognizes the pleasure the Spencers got from buying the Navajo blanket but at the same time fails to value their feelings because he does not believe that they have any. He does not realize that his teacher is concerned for his well-being and is making an effort to help him. He interprets most of Mr Spencer's well-intentioned talk as an attempt to humiliate him. To do him credit, however, Holden is outwardly polite and pleasant. Although he soon wishes he had not paid the visit at all, he tells Mr Spencer he would not have left without saying goodbye.

Whenever he pauses to analyse them, Holden is honest about his reactions. He says openly that he doesn't like being in the presence of illness. He makes no pretence of being concerned or interested in the health of his teacher. The smells of medicine and the dismal appearance of the sick depress him. Further evidence of his dislike of the physical is indicated in his reaction to the sight of old people's bodies. He notices and comments on Mr Spencer's picking his nose, and his inability to throw papers on to the bed. He shuts his mind to what Mr Spencer is trying to say, allowing himself to be preoccupied by the hardness of the bed and the teacher's mannerisms. He doesn't allow Mr Spencer, or, indeed, anybody, to pass beyond his defensive barrier.

Mr Spencer is aware of Holden's remoteness, although Holden fancies that his lack of participation in the conversation is unobserved. The teacher tries to penetrate it, asking how Holden really feels. But Holden senses that he is being probed and drowns Mr Spencer's voice. There is, it seems, nothing that can make him acknowledge a sense of purpose in life.

It is obvious from Holden's examination script that he has learnt nothing about the Egyptians since primary school days, and has taken no interest at all in the lessons. All that he can remember is the mummification process. This immature approach to study is epitomized in his telling Mr Spencer that he has revised so that he will not hurt the teacher's feelings, and in writing the absurd note at the end of the examination essay, solely in order to reassure Mr Spencer that he does not mind failing the history examination. It is apparent that Holden has no idea of work, but that he is a thoughtful person.

At the end of his visit, we are still in sympathy with Holden. It was indeed a dirty trick however well-intentioned, to read out his letter, and a reader of any sensitivity will share with Holden some of his hatred of the sickroom atmosphere and his delight in making his escape from it.

Structurally, this chapter introduces several themes which will be expanded later in the book. The first is Holden's constant, nagging worry about what happens to the ducks in Central Park in the winter. This childish concern brings him into conflict with several people later in the book. It is a fantasy, an escape. He likes to imagine the presence of a kindly man taking the ducks away to safety and warmth.

The second recurring preoccupation mentioned in this chapter is the concept of 'phoniness'. To Holden, insincerity is the greatest sin that exists. Mr Haas, his previous headmaster, is cited as an example of phoniness, talking at greater length for example, to wealthier parents. Holden feels more strongly for others than for himself on occasions, a point in his favour; but his sympathy and indignation are at times misplaced and over-sensitive.

The mention of the Egyptians in the examination paper also ties up with one of Holden's childhood interests, his visits to the museum in Central Park, which has a section devoted to mummies. This will be further explored later in the book with a difference of emphasis.

got a bang out of things (slang) enjoyed doing things.
I don't mean it mean Holden didn't intend being uncharitable.
beat-up Navajo blanket The Navajos are a North American Indian tribe.
Yellowstone Park A huge wild-life park in North West Wyoming, containing volcanic scenery and geysers.
Atlantic Monthly A distinguished American literary magazine.
Vicks nose drops A cold remedy, with a particularly powerful smell of camphor.
nodding routine Mr Spencer's nodding of his head was rhythmic and unvarying.
hot-shots Opportunities.
did you carry Did you study.
Beowulf Beowulf is a long, epic poem in old English.
Lord Randal My Son An anonymous ballad dealing with a young man, Lord Randal, whom his mother finds poisoned after a meal with his sweetheart.
chiffonier Chest of drawers.
cement bed Metaphorically reminding us how hard the bed was.
Shot the bull . . . the old bull Talked insincerely.
too much on opposite sides of the pole Did not understand one another.
and all that crap Holden means they behaved insincerely, shaking hands in a social way.

Chapter 3

The boastful style of the opening sentence sets the mood for the chapter. It is to be one of self-conscious bravado. Although Holden dislikes phoneys, he distinguishes phoniness from lying. Lying he views as a method of self-preservation. Holden is placed in the context of his boarding-school society and relieves the stress of his visit to Mr Spencer by relating an episode showing his independence of authority. We are reminded of his immaturity: Holden shows more appreciation of the crude behaviour of Marsalla in chapel than of the well-intentioned speech of their patron, whom he considers a phoney. He adopts a thoughtlessly cynical style when he talks of the undertaker putting bodies in sacks and dumping them in the river, although in essence Holden is pointing to the fact that there is money to be made from death. He refers scathingly to the idea that Ossenburger might have a religious faith. This attitude of complete self-absorption is extended by the reference to his buying a hat immediately after he had lost the fencing foils. Holden relates the Ossenburger episode, using a great deal of schoolboy cliché and slang which places him firmly in the appreciative ranks of the boys. He exaggerates the length of Ossenburger's speech; he exclaims, to show how cross the headmaster was; he translates the school's particular slang.

The one place he can find privacy and a measure of comfort is the study-bedroom he shares with an older boy, Ward Stradlater. It is interesting that he chooses to settle down with a book by Thomas Hardy. Although he refers several times to his illiteracy, it is clear from his remarks that he not only reads but thinks and forms opinions on books. Holden's views are curiously unformed, but motivated by genuine feeling. He says he prefers books which make him feel that the author is someone to whom he could speak on the telephone. This seems a reasonable and quite a thoughtful way of describing a book which he enjoys reading. This also explains Holden's attitude to the people who read this book, his own. He talks to the reader as a friend, because that is the way he would like to be treated by other authors. At the end of the book, he further explores his enjoyment of digression.

Robert Ackley is the first of Holden's schoolmates to be described. He is eighteen, two years older than Holden. Physically, he disgusts Holden because he doesn't brush his teeth, and has pimples. Ackley admittedly has unpleasant mannerisms such as touching other people's possessions and cleaning and cutting his fingernails in Holden's room, but if anyone's behaviour appears remarkable or odd it is Holden's. Holden doesn't look up when Ackley comes into the room; he mumbles an answer to his questions; he teases him; he won't tell Ackley the name of the book he is reading, and finally he deliberately tries to annoy him by pretending he's blind. This practical, imitative 'horsing around' is the nearest that Holden comes to humour. His intention is less to amuse than to annoy, and in describing it as sadistic he is close to the truth. Holden takes life seriously. He is particularly sour because Ackley laughs when the tennis racquet falls on Holden's head.

The confrontation with Ackley serves to highlight Holden's immature behaviour. Their conversation is characterized by its dullness which reflects Holden's apathetic attitude to the school and to life.

Before his entrance, Holden and Ackley discuss Holden's room-mate Stradlater. We are given two differing viewpoints, and again it is left to us to make up our own minds. Holden stresses Stradlater's generosity and makes it clear that he agrees with Stradlater about Ackley's lack of personal hygiene. Holden gives the impression that Ackley is jealous of Stradlater, who is gregarious and extrovert. Ackley is particularly interested in Stradlater's social life, possibly because he has none of his own, and he comments on Stradlater's conceited, superior attitude.

Stradlater's fleeting appearance is characterized by his speed and decision. He is much more interested in getting ready to go out on a date than in squabbling with the boys. He speaks briefly and to the point. His sentences are short and rapid to match his movements. In every way he is seen as the opposite of Holden and Ackley. His arrival has the effect of energizing the room.

That killed me Holden often uses this phrase to express his amusement or shock.

stiffs Dead bodies.

Out of Africa by Isak Dinesen Isak Dinesen was the pen-name used by Karen Blixen, a Danish story and travel writer. *Out of Africa*, published in 1937, tells of her life in Kenya. She has a gift for evocative narrative.

Ring Lardner Ringold Lardner (1885–1933) was an American storyteller and humorist with a remarkable ear for vernacular speech.

The Return of the Native A novel by Thomas Hardy (see below) published in 1878.

Of Human Bondage A novel by Somerset Maugham, (1874–1965) a storyteller of genius with a sardonic view of human behaviour.

Eustacia Vye The restless, passionate, heroine of *The Return of the Native* by Thomas Hardy (1840–1928). He wrote many poems and novels based on the Wessex countryside.

knock me out Impress.

you were a goner There was no hope of escape.

horsing around Playing the fool.

hound's tooth jacket A woven patterned jacket made of wool.

Chapter 4

The tone of this chapter is vivid; Stradlater's energy and their friendly relationship have an enlivening effect on Holden. At the beginning of this chapter as he watches Stradlater shave, Holden, forced to admire Stradlater's physique and appearance, and secretly a little jealous of him, is struggling to express the difference between superficial and real attractiveness. Stradlater comes into the first category because in spite of using a filthy razor and borrowing Holden's hair oil and jacket he always looks neat and attractive, which Holden feels is unfair.

Stradlater is easy going, accustomed to getting his own way, and demonstrates considerable patience with the antics of his young room-mate. He is agreeable to Holden's going downstairs to say hello to Jane, his date. Holden, compared with his room-mate, can be seen here as he really is; an immature sixteen year old. He is unaware of Stradlater's more adult forbearance. He continually refers to Stradlater's preoccupation with his appearance, which is a stage he has not yet reached and does not fully understand. Holden is aware of his physical inferiority; we have already been reminded both in this chapter and in the last, that Holden is much slighter than Stradlater and less physically fit.

It is ironic in view of his expulsion that Holden should be asked to write a composition, and there is a certain amount of humour to be derived from his bitter reaction. He does not realize that Stradlater was humouring him to persuade him into writing the essay. He thought Stradlater appreciated his tap-dancing. It is also noteworthy that although Holden professes to hate films, he derives pleasure from imitating them.

The news of the identity of Stradlater's date produces a very strong emotional reaction in Holden. He says that he felt close to collapse, and it is easy to understand why. He is aware of his own lack of manhood by comparison with Stradlater; he has a sense of academic failure, and the mention of Jane Gallagher's name reminds him of the strong feelings he had for her. Information about her comes flooding out to Stradlater, to whom she is just an unknown date.

Holden is bored and lonely. He still thinks of her and himself as being two years younger; dwelling on the idea of her having a date with the adult, experienced Stradlater makes Holden apprehensive. It is at this point that the conflict in Holden's mind begins, sparked off by memories of Jane Gallagher, who remains an ideal of innocent, unapproachable girlhood throughout the book.

can Toilet.
chewed the rag Talked.
Song of India A contemporary hit song.
Slaughter on Tenth Avenue A jazzy tune with a strongly marked rhythm.
secret slob Someone who appeared clean and attractive, but who was not totally scrupulous about hygiene.
fixing himself up Washing and shaving, etc.
Year Book American schools and colleges produce annuals with photographs and résumés of all the students.
Be a buddy. Be a buddyroo Stradlater is trying to cajole Holden into helping him.
sink them Score goals.
Ziegfeld Follies A film made in 1944 inspired by the great showman Florenz Ziegfeld (1867–1932). It was a splendid, plotless revue.
B.M. and Shipley Two American women's colleges. Bryn Mawr is the prestigious one.
Vitalis A cream to make the hair lie flat and shine.
Checkers Draughts.

Chapter 5

The restless behaviour of Holden and his friends on Saturday night is typical of adolescents: they cannot bear the idea of staying in, yet they have nothing planned and nowhere to go. Because they have not eaten much at their evening meal, they are quite able to eat a couple of hamburgers, and they are all young enough to enjoy playing around in the snow. Holden in particular is pleased with it for its own sake; he enjoys the childishness of a snowball fight, and wanders around with a snowball until the bus-driver makes him throw it away.

Holden is generous in spirit as well as with his possessions; he lends his jacket to Stradlater and his typewriter to a boy down the hall, and invites Ackley to go to town with him and Brossard because he knows what loneliness is like.

On their return, however, Ackley insists on recounting his sexual fantasies to Holden, who is convinced that Ackley is a virgin. Holden wants to get on with writing the essay for Stradlater. This is an escape to the past, and a source of comfort to Holden as he allows himself to dwell on a subject which he usually keeps deeply hidden, his dead young brother.

At this point, now that we begin to feel we know and like Holden, because of his honesty and his attempts to make sense of the world he lives in, we are told of the single most important event in his life; the event that shaped much of his personality. Three years previously his brother Allie had died of leukemia. It is mentioned with suspicious casualness and half-buried under a morass of apology. That Holden happened to have Allie's baseball mitt with him at boarding school arouses the reader's sympathy and warmth, but we do not begin to understand the full force of Holden's feelings until we read on p.42 of the effect that Allie's death had on him. It is chilling to think that he put enough force into breaking the windows to mutilate his own hand, and the tenderness of his recollections, recounted without self-consciousness, shows the depth of his emotions.

Brown Betty A dessert made from layers of apples and breadcrumbs.
just for a change Holden is being sarcastic. He means Ackley is always in his room.
Buick A large ostentatious car.
baseball mitt To cushion the hand against the ball when fielding.
leukemia A fatal blood cell disorder, in which there are too many white cells in the blood.
Maine, on July 18, 1946 The exact details of Allie's death show how much it means to Holden, who is so imprecise about other matters. Maine is a mountainous forested state in New England, with many holiday areas.

Revision questions on Chapters 1–5

1 Make lists of the things Holden does which are (a) mature and (b) immature. Define 'maturity'. Underline anything he does which you consider hurtful to others.

2 Write a dialogue set in the street outside the subway between Holden and the members of the fencing team.

3 Write an entry in Mr Spencer's diary for the day that Holden went to visit him. Say what Mr Spencer tried to tell Holden and how he thinks Holden reacted to the advice.

4 Define 'phoney'. What sort of behaviour does Holden think of as being phoney? Are there any examples in these first chapters of Holden's being a phoney? How would he justify being a phoney himself when he hates it so much in others?

5 Write about the scene in the bathroom from Stradlater's viewpoint. What is he thinking? Why is he so indifferent to Holden's behaviour? Begin by writing something along the lines of 'Caulfield followed me into the can. . .'

6 What would Holden have mentioned in the essay about Allie's baseball glove? Write the first paragraph as you imagine Holden might have done. Do you think his essay-writing style would be different from the way he writes in the book?

7 Write an account of the interview that took place between Dr Thurmer and Mr and Mrs Caulfield. Mention Holden's family history and previous schools as well as his lack of achievement at Pencey.

8 Write notes on the characters of Ackley, Stradlater and Mr Spencer.

9 How does Holden react to the news that Stradlater is going out with Jane Gallagher and why?

10 Using page 5 of the Penguin edition only, write a list of the information that Holden gives at the start of the book. What conclusions can you draw about his character so far?

11 How does the information about the death of Allie alter our attitude towards Holden? Write one paragraph about how you felt about Holden before you knew of Allie, and another detailing your response to Holden after you heard of Allie.

12 Holden's style is colloquial. Give examples of repetition, cliché, slang, swearing, poor grammar, weak sentence structure and exclamation.

13 Would you prefer it if *The Catcher in the Rye* had been written in a more literary style? Give reasons for your opinion.

Chapter 6

This chapter follows the development of Holden's neurotic fears about Jane Gallagher and illustrates his growing lack of communication with those around him. All evening, Holden has brooded on the progress of Stradlater's date and he has allowed his fears to grow out of proportion. Jane has become a symbol of youthful innocence, envisaged as a small girl caught in the clutches of a sex-fiend. Holden refuses to realize that Jane is now older, a free agent, and that Stradlater is quite a pleasant young man.

Holden can be seen here projecting his own fears about growing up on to his image of Jane. These fears have now filled his mind to the exclusion of all else. When Stradlater returns, Holden's sentences are curt and cold. He is hostile, and waits for his room-mate to mention Jane. He is no longer interested in his jacket. He tears up the essay when Stradlater rejects it because he is concentrating exclusively on his consuming apprehension. Holden is obsessed with a nightmarish fantasy that he can't put a name to and eventually he concentrates all his obsessive worries on the sexual act itself. His voice is shaking when he asks Stradlater about the date.

Their lack of communication is apparent in their attitudes. Stradlater is casual, unaware of Holden's tension. He is playful and jovial in response to Holden's questioning. Holden loses control; all his neuroses culminate in the desire to hurt Stradlater. This moment, if it were not so tense with pent-up emotion, would be an anticlimax indeed. Holden is no match at all for Stradlater. His impotent fury makes him goad Stradlater with words when force is useless, and the inevitable result, although delayed because of Stradlater's innate good-nature, is punitive and final.

Holden is conscious of his own childishness and lack of control, although he does nothing to stop himself from behaving badly. He knows that he is trying to provoke Stradlater right from the start, when he smokes in their room. He knows he is saying outrageous things, but enjoys the sensation of losing all his inhibitions.

Stradlater shows considerable restraint. He has no idea what it is that has made Holden behave like this. He is aware that his young room-mate is hysterical. He treats him as an over-excited child, holding Holden's wrists, telling him to be quiet, warning him several times to stop. Once the fight is over, Holden continues to behave like a child – he refuses to get up off the floor; he won't stop delivering petty taunts; he rather regrets that he didn't fracture his skull to spite Stradlater, and once the coast is clear he is fascinated by the sight of his bloodied face in the mirror. In search of yet more attention, he then goes to exhibit himself to Ackley.

We have been shown Holden in action, and a miserable picture it is, but his behaviour touches a chord of recognition in all of us.

griping Complaining.
socks Small, light blows.
faculty Staff.
Give her the time Have sexual intercourse.
in the toothbrush In the mouth.
that injury I told you about The hand he pushed through the garage windows the night Allie died.
I'm not too tough. I'm a pacifist Holden seems to equate the one with the other, unconsciously ironic humour.

Chapter 7

The sensation of a room in darkness is well evoked through the use of a few telling examples. Holden slips on a shoe, he can't find the light switch, and the ghostly appearance of Ackley's spot cream is well noted.

Although Holden has gone to Ackley for some companionship and attention, he doesn't really want to communicate with him. His feelings are running too deep. He behaves just as badly as Ackley did to him earlier. He won't tell Ackley what the fight was about, and he doesn't listen to Ackley's well-intentioned advice about staunching the bleeding. Holden enjoys the sensation of being tough, and playing down the fight. When Ackley loses interest Holden is deprived of his audience and is ironically rude.

Holden is obsessed with the idea of Stradlater's sexuality and Jane as the victim of his lust. His imagination is fired by memories of Stradlater's persuasively seductive technique on an occasion when they double-dated in the very car Stradlater used that night. Holden's agitation is very real; his feelings of despair are overwhelming; but it must be observed that there is no basis for such a strongly emotional response. Jane Gallagher was never more than a friend to Holden. She is now two years older and may welcome Stradlater's advances.

What Holden is upset about is something within himself; the development of his own sexual impulses, which he cannot control and therefore wishes to mask, and the loss of boyhood innocence which is associated with his dead brother Allie and childhood. He projects hatred and fear on to Stradlater because he sees in the eighteen-year-old the man he will soon become, and also the embodiment of the sexual appetite which he fears and relishes at the same time. He even wonders, briefly, about bcoming a monk.

His decision to opt out of Pencey is understandable, in view of his conflicting feelings. He is lonely, friendless, an academic failure. His nature is impulsive. He has told nobody of his plans.

It should be understood at this point that Holden was accustomed to moving in wealthy circles. Later on in the book there will be more examples, but remember the stolen camel's hair coat and fur-lined gloves. He still had a reversible coat and a jacket that even the rich Stradlater wanted to borrow. He wore sheepskin slippers. Pencey was an expensive private school. His typewriter was a good one. He didn't need to worry about possessions or money, and, living away from home, he was used to making many of his own decisions.

Even his departure from Pencey was an anticlimax; a study in futility. Already sad at the thought of his mother's disappointment, after shouting his defiant farewell to wake up all the boys, he slipped and fell on the stairs.

Canasta A card game of the rummy type originating in South America.
What a witty guy . . . He was the perfect host, boy Two examples of Holden's ironic comments on Ackley's lack of hospitality.
to snow someone i.e. persuade; seduce.
Abraham Lincoln Born in Kentucky 1809 he became President in 1861. The phrase, 'Government of the People, by the people, for the people' comes from his Gettysburg speech of 1863. He was assassinated in 1865.
Gladstones A travelling bag with flexible sides hinged so as to open flat into two separate compartments. Named after W. E. Gladstone (1809–1898) Prime Minister of England between 1868 and 1894.
Spaulding's Sports shop.
wad A roll of paper money.

Chapter 8

This chapter begins with Holden experiencing inertia and depression as an aftermath of his earlier hysterical outburst. It must be around midnight as he waits for the train, but time has no meaning for him. Holden remarks on the cold as he did in the first chapter, a reminder of the theft of his coat, and also of his physical state. His face is bruised and covered in blood which he had half-heartedly wiped off with a handful of snow. He is too depressed to enjoy the ride or read a magazine. The writing is subdued and static to reflect Holden's state of mind.

Holden enjoys the company of women, and finds attraction in details that others might find annoying; for example, his comment that women often leave their luggage in the aisle where others can trip over it. He seizes on the arrival of Ernest Morrow's mother as a diversion from the lassitude of his own mind. He finds her attractive and enjoys a mild flirtation with her, indulging his imagination and letting his invention run riot. He has already mentioned his tendency to tell lies, and begins by giving her a false name; that of the janitor. This is a magnificent and astonishing idea which is quite audacious in its simplicity. It will immediately be obvious to her son, or any of the boys, who it was she was speaking to. Inspired by this, the rest of their conversation builds up to heights of burlesque effrontery. He answers her questions about Pencey enigmatically, and tells her a series of lies, each one improving on the last, about her son's popularity and sensitivity at school. Holden thus transmutes the dislike he feels for Ernest into a very personal humour. The negative emotion is recharged as a positive imaginative entity.

The wit lies more in the concept than in the detail. There are a few memorable remarks, such as the comparison of Ernest Morrow to a toilet seat, and the idea that his mother should have carried a telephone round with her.

Throughout the conversation she treats him as an adult; even when he offers her cigarettes in a non-smoker compartment and drinks though he is visibly underage, she only remonstrates gently. Holden thinks she probably suspects the truth about her son's behaviour, and in a way he regrets deceiving her, but he cannot resist a captive audience. Here is the attention he failed to command in the dormitory and he makes the most of it.

Holden doesn't tell her the truth about anything; he says his nose is bleeding because he was hit by a snowball; he tells her he has a brain tumour, and that he is going to visit his grandmother in South America. Once he gets started, he cannot stop lying. This is immature behaviour but it represents a desire to improve upon reality. Holden tells Ernest's mother pleasant things; the things a mother would be pleased to hear about her son.

The interlude in the train marks the boundary between the

world of school and New York. It is appropriate to regard it as a transition.

laid one on me Hit me.
in the sack In bed.
was she lousy with rocks She was wearing a lot of jewellery.
as sensitive as a toilet seat An inspired and degrading simile.
the elections Holden refers to the class voting for form leaders and
  representatives.
was I chucking it Holden was telling wildly improbable lies.
this tiny little tumour on the brain Any brain tumour is a cause for
  concern. The size is immaterial.

Chapter 9

It is typical of Holden's confused state of mind that he both wishes for company and also to be alone. It is not until he walks into the telephone booth at the station that he begins to realize that the people he would most like to talk to would let his parents know where he is, and that he has nothing to say to either Carl Luce or Jane Gallagher's mother. But he deals with his thoughts on each person separately and never pauses to consider that in many ways he is simply finding excuses for his inaction. At this point, his yearning for attention and his need for solitude are equally balanced. It takes twenty minutes of inward struggle for solitude to win.

Several people are listed at this point, in the order in which Holden loves them. His writer brother DB who was mentioned at the beginning of the book is closely followed by his sister Phoebe. Then comes Jane Gallagher, whose symbolic importance is now high in Holden's thoughts, and Sally Hayes, whose photograph was on his chiffonier at Pencey. Lastly the name Carl Luce is mentioned, but instantly rejected.

It is wryly amusing to observe Holden's determination to communicate being quashed by the monosyllabic taxi-driver. He hesitantly and with much repetition mentions the plight of the ducks in winter which seems to be a theme he calls upon when all else fails, but the driver is unimpressed. He pursues the conversation and even invites the driver for a drink on the way, but is rebuffed. Holden tries to imitate the clichés that he imagines taxi-drivers might use, but he does not realize how juvenile he must sound. On the contrary, he imagines that he appears quite sophisticated, and asks the driver the name of the musicians playing at various hotels. Even this overture to the superior knowledge of the driver is ignored, so Holden has no option but to relinquish the conversation with a sarcastic sneer to himself. That the taxi driver simply does not consider Holden worthy of his notice, simply does not occur to Holden.

The glimpse of other people's lives from the hotel window makes Holden think about sex. He acknowledges that he doesn't understand it, and yet it fascinates him. He tries to define a series of rules to follow, which hinge around the idea that it is defiling to have sex with people one doesn't like; but Holden seems incapable of following his own rules, however admirable. Although he immediately thinks of Jane Gallagher he finds a reason for not contacting her – ashamed of the power of his own emotions which could possibly get out of control. Instead, he breaks his newly formulated rule and telephones a woman whom he thinks is a prostitute.

The telephone call to Faith Cavendish is another rejection. It starts off badly, probably because it is by now very late and Faith Cavendish was asleep. She is in no mood to play Holden's games, but it is interesting to note that his casual mention of Princeton with all the wealth and connections that the name implies, stems the tide of her annoyance and mellows her. But she is perceptive enough to notice Holden's youth and she does not seem over-interested in meeting him. She fabricates a suffering room-mate when she hears that he is in a telephone-box rather than in an apartment. Holden has been far too adolescently impulsive in telephoning her in the middle of the night, but it is unlikely that Faith Cavendish would have had much time for him, in any case. The telephone call leaves Holden feeling more isolated.

breaking a goddam leg A visually effective way of conveying haste.
Taft, New Yorker Two nightclubs.
I'm loaded I have plenty of money.
He certainly was good company Another of Holden's sarcastic remarks intended to convey the opposite.
screwball Someone weird.
what a gorgeous job Another sarcastic remark.
very crumby stuff Sexual antics.
burlesque stripper A striptease dancer in a nightclub.
Sixty-fifth and Broadway Quite a large junction at the S.W. end of Central Park where Broadway crosses at an angle to 65th Street.
Princeton One of the most prestigious universities in USA.

getting an English accent Becoming cool and remote.
Boy, I *really* fouled that up Spoiled it or made a mess of it. There is
  almost a note of relief in Holden's voice as though he subconsciously
  wanted to avoid meeting her.

Chapter 10

At the beginning of this chapter, Holden speaks to the reader as
to a friend. He is evidently very attached to his sister Phoebe
although she is six years younger than he is, and gives a remarkably detailed picture of her. He admires her high grades in
school and remarks without rancour that he is the only one
without brains in the family. He feels protective and parentally
proud of her. He has made much of her and she is very like a
companion to him in spite of the difference in their ages. He
takes her to films and admires her precocious imitations of
them. The colour of her hair reminds him of Allie's. His mind
dwells on the past again, as he thinks of the Sundays in the park
when he, Allie and Phoebe used to sail Allie's boat. However this
time memories do not arouse a storm of emotion; reassured, he
concentrates more on the present and the search for further
diversion. Holden has found in the prospect of action a cure for
his depression.

His memories of Phoebe and the mention of her mis-spelling
the name of her heroine are endearing because they are so true
to life. He remarks on odd details about people – Phoebe's white
gloves, for instance, or the rings on Ernest's mother's hands. He
notices the provincial hats that the three 'girls' are wearing.

In this chapter it is apparent that Holden regards himself as
being much more adult than his years. He is so sure of himself
that he is not in the least perturbed by others, and he is generous
and gentlemanly to a fault; he has higher standards than the
three women he entertains; he is judging them and noticing
what they say and do all the time he is with them. He is amused
that the two ugly ones don't want to resemble one another; he
knows it is not sophisticated to drink Tom Collinses in midwin-
ter; he finds Marty's coy references to 'the little girls' room' very
boring, and disagrees with her enthusiasm for the clarinet
player, whom he considers ordinary.

Although Holden imagines that he is suave and adult, the
waiter refuses to sell him alcohol and the three women at the
adjoining table find it very amusing that he is trying to flirt with

them. Holden perseveres, though. He does not let their behaviour upset him; he assumes that they are ignorant and stupid because they laugh at him; he has self-confidence. Bernice, the blonde woman whom he prefers is not listening to what he is saying or paying attention to him at all while they are dancing. Holden assumes that this is because she is really stupid; he does not wonder if it is because she does not find him charming. He has to ask her three times where she comes from, and she finds his constant swearing offensive. The three women are constantly looking round the room while Holden is with them; Holden assumes that this is because they are searching for movie stars because they are so provincial, but it is likely that they are looking for adult male company.

The author successfully conveys the atmosphere of a second-rate nightclub, with its seedy customers and uninspiring music.

She's psychic His mother can tell if one of her children is around.
The Baker's Wife *La Femme du Boulanger* is one of Marcel Pagnol's films, a pleasant comedy about village life. (1938).
Raimu (1883–1946) His real name was Jules Muraire, a French character actor with a music-hall background.
The Thirty-Nine Steps Holden is probably referring to Hitchcock's 1935 version which hit the authentic note of Buchan's book with its touches of macabre comedy and romantic banter.
Robert Donat (1905–1958) A distinguished British actor of Polish descent with a very melodious voice.
I should've waved a buck i.e. should have bribed him.
strictly from hunger i.e. although the women were not attractive to him, he needed their attention.
grools One of Holden's words implying stupidity and ugliness.
tricky stuff Difficult steps.
Peter Lorre (1901–1964) A highly individual (Hollywood) Hungarian character actor with big eyes and hesitant manner.
A *queen*, for Chrissake Holden sarcastically refers to Bernice's dislike of his swearing.
Seattle, Washington A spit of land between Puget Sound and Lake Washington.
jitterbugging A very fast dance of the period.
a flock of goddam movie stars Holden ironically overstates.
The Stork Club – El Morocco Well-known nightclubs frequented by celebrities.
Gary Cooper (1901–1961) American leading filmstar who spoke slowly and acted the parts of honest, determined men.
nearly committed suicide Holden's overstatement of their excitement.

Tom Collinses A cocktail mixed with gin, sugar, lemon or lime juice and soda water.

ice-cold hot licks i.e. the clarinet player's solo part.

she was certainly witty Holden means the opposite – his usual irony.

Radio City Music Hall In New York, where all the radio and television shows are recorded.

Revision questions on Chapters 6–10

1 What led up to Holden's decision to leave Pencey? Do you think it was a wise decision in the circumstances?

2 Write a letter from Mrs Morrow to her son Ernest detailing the meeting on the train with Rudolf Schmidt (Holden).

3 Write a telephone conversation between Mrs Morrow and Dr Thurmer in which she mentions the meeting with Rudolf Schmidt (Holden) and he gradually realizes who she is talking about.

4 Write a short scene from a play including the conversation that the three women have about Holden when they get back to their room.

5 What have we found out about Phoebe so far? (Include information from the first five chapters as well). How can you tell Holden loves her?

6 Write an entry from Faith Cavendish's diary including the evening that Holden telephoned her.

7 List the events of Holden's day so far in chronological order and put an approximate time by each. Update it as you go on through the book.

8 Holden becomes gradually more ironic in Chapters 6–10. Give some examples of his increasing use of sarcasm.

9 Go through Chapter 6, outlining the various ways in which Holden and Stradlater fail to communicate.

10 From Chapter 8, write out all the facts you are told about Ernest Morrow. Then in a further paragraph, list the lies that Holden tells.

11 Go through Chapter 10 in detail, writing out the events in the Lavender Room, trying to separate the characters of the three women.

12 What have we added to our knowledge of Holden in these last five chapters? Has your opinion of him altered in any way?

Chapter 11

This chapter marks a pause in the action, in which Holden reminisces about Jane, and the reader is allowed to know why she is held up as an ideal. The contrast of past happiness balances present misery.

Holden is calmer and admits that it is unlikely that Stradlater actually had intercourse with Jane that evening. Now that he is away from the claustrophobic atmosphere of the boarding school, such fantasies have receded, and are replaced by pleasant reminiscences of the summer that he and Jane had spent two years before.

Again, it is the details that conjure up the atmosphere of that summer. The Dobermann, the number of golf balls Jane managed to lose, the way she shut her eyes when swinging the club and the sad rubbing of her tear into the checker board are all vivid. The most memorable one is mentioned to Stradlater in Chapters 4 and 6: that she kept her kings in the back row. We learn little of Jane herself. All that we know of her is presented to us through the filter of Holden's recollections. The image is of a youthful association in a wealthy neighbourhood, tennis and golf, both, incidentally still prestige sports in America today. They went swimming and to the cinema together and when it rained they would play checkers. We are not given any physical information about Jane, except that she had a large mouth, and was not a pretty girl. Her reticence is conveyed; she does not confide exactly why she is crying. Their relationship was not physical, but Holden loved her.

Holden's protective instincts were aroused by Jane. She had a tense relationship with her stepfather who, according to what Holden told Stradlater on page 36, drank too much, and never wore more than a pair of shorts around the house. He was supposed to be a writer, but all that Holden noticed him doing was listening to radio mystery plays.

The charm of this reverie is intensified by contrast with the deserted lobby and the revolting chair. Holden is now ready to face the world.

vomity-looking chair The adjective presumably applies more to the colour of the chair than to its condition, but 'vomity' aptly conveys the seediness of the hotel.
made a big stink about it Whether intentional or not, this is a pun.
conversed Holden occasionally mixes his idioms. This formality is not in his usual style.
Eight The repetition of the number gives it emphasis. It is a lot of golf balls to lose.
muckle-mouthed Her mouth was large and mobile.
booze hound Alcoholic.
glider A swinging chair with an awning.
He's so good he's amost corny Ernie has reached such perfection that he makes his piano-playing sound too easy.

Chapter 12

This chapter falls into complementary halves; the taxi ride and Ernie's night club. They are both unpleasant experiences for Holden, and reinforce the idea that he is a child masquerading in an adult world whose rules he does not understand; he constantly finds himself at odds with those he meets. People are not particularly unpleasant to Holden; the problem lies within himself.

At the beginning of the chapter, reassured by his memories of Jane, Holden longs for the peace of home and the company of Phoebe. But his fear of his parents is still too strong to allow him to return. Holden's next encounter and complete failure to communicate are well depicted; Horwitz the cab driver is unprepared for the subject-matter and it takes him some time to adjust mentally. He is not very intelligent; Holden has to repeat himself, and explain several times what he means. Horwitz is excitable and short-tempered. His first reaction is to snap and swear when presented with an idea he can't understand. He shouts at Holden and behaves very aggressively, turning round in his seat to force his opinions home, ignoring the driving, and behaving in an extreme, almost unbalanced way. He appears to listen to only half of what Holden says to him, and at first completely misunderstands Holden's question, shouting at him about the fish, not the ducks. He then shows a lamentable belligerence and ignorance about fish. This Horwitz ordeal is more upsetting to Holden than he confesses even to himself. Its force is only perceived at the beginning of the following chapter, when he walks the forty-one blocks back to his hotel rather than get into a similar taxicab situation.

This represents a confrontation with the less rarefied, seamier side of life for Holden, who is used to the expensive seclusion of school and home. New York cab drivers have a reputation for their belligerent behaviour, and Horwitz is a prime example of the type. Holden, who had asked the question as a diversion and means of conversation, finds himself regretting it, as the taxi driver becomes personal and nasty.

This confrontation has its foundation firmly in black comedy. Set in a taxi in the middle of the night, the concept of Holden and Horwitz trying but failing to communicate on such an extraordinary subject is a study in character analysis. The way in which Horwitz returns time and again to the subject of the fish when Holden obviously wishes to drop it shows his doggedly obtuse intention to get the better of the argument, and his final utterance and disappearance at high speed indicate that Horwitz is intent on having the final word. Even Holden's grim summation of Horwitz's character is darkly amusing. The two of them are entrenched in their own worlds with their own preconceptions. For Holden this represents another link in the chain of people he cannot relate to.

Once Holden enters the night club he is in another stratum of society; surrounded by those to whom he socially belongs, but whom he regards as phoney. There is nothing he likes about the night club, a fact he admits with honesty. He dislikes the crowd of college and prep school people who are there, and is caustic about the respectful attention that Ernie's piano playing evokes from the crowd of fans. Holden is quick to attack anything he considers pretentious; he remarks on the mirror that reflects not Ernie's hands, as would have been appropriate, but his face. He notices the embellishments that Ernie adds to the music, making it sound more complicated than it is. Holden reacts cynically to the undiscerning applause of the onlookers. He views the entire entertainment in terms too simplistic and rigid to appreciate that Ernie's respectful, humble bow denotes his acceptance of the applause, with no reference to his self-esteem. Holden feels that Ernie can no longer gauge his own true worth as a piano player; again, Holden is projecting his own interpretation on to others.

And, with that warring mixture of feelings that characterizes him, he realizes that, though he is disgusted by Ernie's showmanship, he does not wish to leave, and return to the brooding solitude of the hotel.

With endearing adolescent inconsistency Holden resents the ease with which he manages to be served with alcohol; it is clear at this point that nothing is going to please him. The various other diners are commented on without the sympathy that he showed earlier in the evening; fatigue and depression are taking their toll. He can't find anything attractive at all about the ugly girl at the next table.

Judging by his behaviour all evening, his loneliness and searching for company, particularly female company, it is surprising that Holden does not value the chance encounter with Lillian. He professes to find her a phoney, but he had managed to put up with the uninspiring company of Bernice and her two friends earlier on in the evening. It could be that he is jealous of his brother DB, and dislikes Lillian because she is obviously hoping he will mention her to his brother. Or perhaps he really finds her unappealing. It would seem most likely that he knows he will be unable to compete with the attentions of the manly naval officer escorting her and consequently pretends an indifference he does not feel. Having made the excuse, Holden feels he must leave and, though he was far from enjoying the evening at Ernie's, feels a sullen annoyance that they have spoiled his fun.

tossed his cookies Been sick.
shoot the bull Talk.
Quite amusing and all One of Holden's sarcastic comments.
stinking it up Showing off his expertise.
frozen daiquiries An elegant sorbet-style fruity drink often rum-based.
Joe Yale Upper-class university student.
tattersall vests Brightly striped or checked waistcoats.
Ivy League bastards Students at the most upper-class universities.
crocked Drunk.
prize horse's ass Fool.
knockers Breasts.
don't break around forty of your fingers Another of Holden's exaggerations. He refers to the strength of a handshake.

Chapter 13

This chapter further illustrates the gap between reality and Holden's fantasies. It begins by exploring the extent of his cowardice. He does not acknowledge his reason for walking back to the hotel, but explains away his decision with the transparent excuse that he is tired of taxis. He thinks about the theft of his gloves at Pencey and fantasizes situations in which he shows cowardice – he realizes that he assumes indifference to mask his inferiority when faced with more resolute people. The clear-sightedness is immediately followed by several examples of the blurring that Holden must overcome if he is to grow up. He says he had to force himself to be sick after drinking in chapel, instead of admitting the truth. He is afraid to go into the bar after meeting a couple of men who inhibit him. He doesn't have the strength of character to resist the pimp in the lift and simply say no to his suggestion of a prostitute.

The episode with the prostitute is one of the most memorable in the book. It demonstrates Holden's extreme youth, his inability to match performance with fantasy and his genuine likeableness in spite of some rather annoying characteristics. It is honest of Holden to admit his own naiveté right from the start, when he is unsure of what the lift-boy is asking him. This is disarming and makes us feel in sympathy with him in what could prove to be an unnerving experience. Structurally the book has been leading up to this point from the start with its mentions of sexual adventure, its comparison of Holden's inexperience and Stradlater's savoir faire, Holden's titillation and emotional storm at the thought of Jane Gallagher. We are prepared to share Holden's first sexual encounter following the indications earlier in the book.

We have been reminded continually that his emotional development is inconsistent. It would be most traumatic for him to have to cope with any further experiences. As though he senses this, Holden immediately regrets having agreed to have a prostitute at all. But he is too weak to lose face by declining at this stage.

Before the prostitute arrives, he explains away his virginity in a confused way. Holden feels deprived, but with a wonderful shift to optimism thinks that the prostitute will at least give him the opportunity of practising his sexual skills. The humour of the clichéd pseudo-erotic literature he has read is compounded by his naively honest admission that when it comes to dating he is never too sure what he is looking for.

The prostitute is cool and hard; there is great contrast between her unconcerned ease and Holden's determinedly forced nonchalance. Holden has no experience to match her professionalism; all he knows of prostitutes is drawn from literature. His pseudonym is disregarded, his assumption of six additional years disbelieved, and his desperate wish to delay the moment of confrontation treated with suspicion and finally contempt. Holden has now entangled himself in the adult world to such an extent that he must inevitably lose face in order to extricate himself. He is searching for love; she is selling sex.

Two things motivate his refusal to proceed. Once he begins to consider the prostitute as an individual he can no longer consider her a commodity and he finds her pitiful instead of seductive. Also, he still considers sex dirty. Her attempts to arouse him he finds crude.

If nothing else however, Holden has gained from that depressing scene the courage to stand up to her, and he does so twice although he finds her quite formidable. He is not so cowardly as he supposes.

Forty-one gorgeous blocks The effect of the word 'gorgeous' instead of one of Holden's usual epithets brings home his disgust at the distance.

I hardly didn't even show it A mixed-up, childish way of saying he hardly showed he was drunk. This reflects Holden's immaturity.

a little tail Sex.

a throw A single encounter.

polo coat Reefer jacket.

Like fun you are As Holden remarks, this is a childish way of expressing disbelief.

clavichord Holden uses as inappropriate word because he is trying to bluff his way out of the situation. He isn't referring to any specific anatomical part.

Mel-vine Douglas Sunny's pronunciation of Melvyn Douglas (1901–) a suavely elegant film star.

she started getting funny . . . and all The prostitute is trying to arouse him, but Holden finds her efforts offensive.

I was a little premature in my calculations Holden adopts a formal, adult idiom to end the encounter.

spooky Frightening.

crumb-bum Another childish insult.

Chapter 14

Lacking any formal religious belief, Holden has only Allie to call upon in moments of deep need. He does this again at the end of the book. Thoughts of Allie, which though sad are reassuring, remind him of childhood and the continuing sense of his brother's presence. Then he thinks, naturally enough in such a context, of religion. He is by no means an atheist. Just as he has to think of books as messages in which the author is speaking directly to him and may be telephoned, so he responds to the figure of Jesus as to a contemporary, shackled by blundering Disciples who hindered Him. He instinctively grasps the central truth of Jesus's message, just as he has a feeling for the essential core of literature.

The further humiliation Holden has to undergo at the hands of the unpleasant pair shows that he has evoked forces he cannot control in this hostile adult world. They are seedy and sordid. Maurice is a bully. Not content with extorting money he enjoys abusing Holden physically. He did in fact originally ask for only five dollars; Sunny's taking another five out of his wallet is theft in spite of her denial. Ironically Holden did not even get his money's worth for the initial sum. It is noticeable that he cannot admit this failure of manhood to the distasteful Maurice.

Holden emerges from the confrontation quite creditably. He puts up a more convincing defence than he envisaged during the lonely forty-one block walk back to the hotel, in spite of his fear. His voice is shaking, but he does not give in, and it takes physical violence for the pair to get into the room at all. Holden is taking a stand on principle, as he has until now shown little interest in money. Although he does not fight back, in spite of his pain he continues to abuse Maurice verbally until he is knocked flat on the floor. This is a repetition of the conclusion of his earlier fight with Stradlater, which he is quick to appreciate.

This time, his reaction is a flight into fantasy. There is no Ackley to appreciate his 'toughness'. He imagines a violent alternative ending to the fight, and festoons it with the image of Jane Gallagher. This is a merciful release. His imagination is his escape and his healing. Reality at this point is too hurtful to bear. In spite of his hatred of the movies, they serve a useful purpose.

Lake Sedebego A small lake in Maine.
BB guns Ball-bearing guns for which no licence is needed.

I'm sort of an atheist This qualification of a statement which does not
 admit of qualification shows Holden's essential indecisiveness.
that lunatic . . . in the tombs Holden probably refers to the man
 mentioned in Mark, 5, 1–20, whom Jesus cured of demonic
 possession.
chisel Extort money.
Old Maurice had plugged me Holden is fantasizing that Maurice had
 shot him.
rubbernecks Tourists, sightseers.

Chapter 15

Just as after the meeting with the three women in the Lavender
room Holden had a peaceful interlude, here too he is tem-
porarily allowed a respite from his problems. He makes arrange-
ments to meet Sally. He refers casually to necking her, as though
to prove to himself that he is indeed knowledgeable about sex.
Although he despises Sally, and considers her pretentious and
stupid, he needs company. His desire for communication with
others is at the root of much of his behaviour. Note that in her
case he is prepared to put up with her falsity because solitude
would be an unpalatable alternative, and because he finds her
attractive. It is also interesting that he quickly brushes aside the
idea of telephoning Jane Gallagher. He has had enough of
emotion for the present. Sally is evidently easy to deal with;
Holden issues commands and she acquiesces. He shows no affection for her and is cynical about the men whom she says are
wanting to date her. Their meeting is set for a matinée performance, and with that to look forward to, Holden is ready to leave
the hotel.

Not surprisingly, he intends to avoid meeting Maurice but he
still uses the elevator instead of being tempted to go down the
stairs. This represents a modest advance in bravery. He does not
have the heart, however, to check into another hotel after the
Maurice episode, and he still cannot face returning home to his
parents. Resourcefully, he puts his cases into left luggage at
Grand Central Station until he can make a decision.

Several themes are discusssed here; Holden's attitude to
money is examined as he now notices that he has little of it left.
His father is a wealthy corporation lawyer who invests in shows
on Broadway. Holden appears to consider this justification
enough for his own spendthrift behaviour. His lack of a feeling

of personal responsibility also comes through strongly in his remark that he knows his mother will be distressed to hear of his expulsion. It does not occur to him that he could have avoided this by working a little harder at school. He insists on making quite a large donation to the nuns. This continues the theme of prodigality, and also reinforces the idea that Holden was arguing with Maurice the previous night about the principle involved, not the actual amount. It seems inconsistent that he should give away ten dollars immediately after noticing that his money supply was dwindling, but this is an example of Holden's idealism. He acts in accordance with his views, no matter what the cost. Another explanation, supported later in the book, is that he has now made a subconscious decision to rid himself of material goods, as a means of renouncing the world. At the end of the chapter he remarks that money makes him sad.

Holden next explores the nature of friendship. He explains it in terms of symbols he can understand: the difference between his expensive luggage and a room-mate's cheap cases. He thinks it is necessary for people to find equality before they can properly communicate or feel at ease with one another. Pettiness can sour relationships. He implies that people of the same social standing find it easier to get along, even if they are incompatible in other, deeper ways. He mentions Stradlater as an example. This can be taken as a justification of his asking Sally Hayes to the theatre. He does not really like her, but they come from the same social class.

The last theme in this chapter concerns religion: Holden's remarks about Catholicism continue a theme which has been present throughout the book. Holden cannot come to terms with religion, particularly after the death of his brother, yet he is aware that it is a strong force that fascinates him. He is afraid the nuns will ask him if he is a Catholic, almost as if he feels guilty because he is not. If he could find some alternative explanation for the problems of life and death, perhaps he would not be so obsessed with religion. But he cannot accept the faith; he feels that it is like a society in which the members derive pleasure from associating with one another, and from which he is excluded. Holden, predictably cannot consider the nuns as representatives of the Roman Catholic Church, but can only see them as two women, pitiably human, with unbecoming spectacles and a propensity for dropping things. He enjoys talking to them, as they are straightforward and honest. They are people who are certainly not phoney. He wonders how nuns approach some of the topics and personalities in literature, particularly of course, the love scenes. This embarrasses Holden, who cannot bring himself to broach the subject with them at all. Insead he concentrates on his own highly idiosyncratic view of *Romeo and Juliet*. He is not as interested in the star-crossed lovers as in Mercutio, man of action, non-stop talker. His apportioning of blame for Mercutio's death is further evidence of his immaturity. He is correct when he surmises that the nuns wish to stop discussing the play. It is evident he has little of value to say.

Benefits Charity shows.

Grand Sally uses the same word as Mr Spencer. Holden has already remarked how much he hates it.

rushing hell . . . his throat over her Over-dramatizations of ardent courtship.

West Point cadet A student at the American Military Academy near New York. This is a prestigious College.

Grand Central Station The main transport interchange and rail terminus in New York City.

Biltmore A New York hotel.

haul it in Are well paid.

168th Street or 186th Street Poor, lower class areas.

Hardy See note on Chapter 3.

Grendel The name of the monster in *Beowulf* (Refer to note on Chapter 2) which eats the Norsemen.

Mercutio . . . Tybalt . . . Montagues, Capulets All characters in Shakespeare's *Romeo and Juliet*

physicals Medical examinations.

the Nationals at Forest Hills Tennis matches played at the West Side Tennis Club in the central Queens borough.

blue as hell Very sad.

Revision questions on Chapters 11–15

1 Write a letter that Jane Gallagher might have written two years ago, when she was thirteen, telling a school friend about the summer holiday she is spending. Give her opinion of Holden, and relate all the things they do during the holidays.

2 Can you think of any reasons why Holden has such difficulty in talking to cab-drivers? Why does he bring out the worst in them? (Refer to Chapter 9 as well as to Chapter 12 in your answer)

3 Comment on the various types of phoniness that annoy Holden at Ernie's.

4 At the beginning of Chapter 13 Holden depicts his cowardice in great detail. Look at each move he says he will make, then at the end of Chapter 14, where the incident with Maurice is described. Do you think he reacts exactly as he has predicted?

5 Describe the conversation between Sunny and Maurice after she left Holden's room. Use dialogue form. What was her opinion of Holden? Why did Maurice decide to extort more money from him?

6 What are the main differences between the end of the fight with Stradlater and the end of the fight with Maurice? How does Holden react in both cases? (The fight with Stradlater is on pages 48–49).

7 Does Sunny behave as you would expect a prostitute to? What does she do or say that makes you realize she is an individual? Why does she become so angry with Holden?

8 Examine the beginning of Chapter 14 (pages 104, 105), the meeting with the nuns on pages 115–20, and then turn back to page 45. What does Holden know about religion? What is his attitude to it?

9 Holden mentions several books and a type of magazine story. Write what he says about the various books he has read. Use pages 22, 57, 116, 117.

10 What have we learned so far about Sally Hayes and Holden's opinion of her? Look at pages 24, 63, 111, 112.

11 Update the time chart for Holden and his movements.

12 What, in your opinion, is the most significant event that has happened to Holden so far? Explain why you think this.

Chapter 16

This chapter further conveys the difference between the world of adults, which Holden does not wish to enter – because of what he perceives as its phoniness – and the world of childhood, from which he is now excluded because of his age. The two worlds are explored and contrasted, using the various characters Holden meets as representatives of one or the other.

Holden tries to define what it is that he appreciates so much about the nuns, and comes to the conclusion that he likes their complete disregard of themselves and their appearance. He contrasts his own mother, his aunt and Sally Hayes's mother unfavourably with them. His love of the natural, unglamorized aspect of things is further reinforced by his remarks about the record he wants to buy for his sister Phoebe and the happiness he feels in watching the little boy. The child, totally absorbed in his own world, humming 'Coming through the rye' as he walks his straight line in the gutter, is for Holden a reminder of innocence; the quality he holds most precious. The little boy makes Holden feel happier, though all the adults he has come into contact with have made him depressed and reluctant to join their conspiracy of phoniness. He now has a great need to be with Phoebe, his own gateway into childhood. He is delighted to be able to buy her a record he knows will please her.

Holden does not like what he has seen of the adult world. He is depressed by the cinema queues; movies are not a substitute for life. He cannot bear to speak to Jane Gallagher's mother when she answers the telephone, although this could be an excuse for not facing the adult emotions that Jane arouses in him.

When he buys theatre tickets he muses on the hypocrisy of acting, and finds the same fault that he found with Ernie the piano-player. If actors are good, Holden thinks them conceited and artificial. He can hardly concentrate on a play for fear that the actors are going to behave phonily. Phoebe is his guide for what is acceptable, feels 'right', and what is not – he cites the naturalness of Olivier's Hamlet patting a dog, and Ophelia's behaviour with Laertes.

Notice that Holden is becoming more adult – he is beginning to realize that he is getting short of money, and thinks of taking subways instead of taxis, though at the end of the chapter he conveniently forgets to do so; secondly, that he views the park with unsentimental eyes, seeing the place he regarded as a haven in his youth objectively now, as dirty and barren, with unpleasant-looking benches.

He is now regarded as an outsider by the children in the park; they are polite but dismissive to him. The laconic conversation of children is accurately reported. There is no curiosity in the little girl whose skate he tightens. She has to go and meet her friend, and the children on the seesaw don't want him to join in their game. This does not depress Holden, for he has no desire to be a child again; he wants to carry clear childhood vision into adult life.

He realizes that he is an adult when he finds he has no desire to re-enter the Natural History Museum. Athough he has vivid memories of class trips there, of the teacher and the various children and their exploits, he is aware that the static quality of the museum contrasts with the changing nature of life. The feeling of childhood excursions is well conveyed, in the noise and commotion of the marbles bouncing on the polished floor, the sticky hands of a childhood partner and the mention of the rainbows in the puddles outside.

Sally Hayes' crazy mother Holden uses the word 'crazy' quite meaninglessly here.

Dixieland Strongly rhythmic and melodious jazz music.

look sharp Neat, well-dressed.

'If a body catch a body' The title of the book is reflected in the mistaken words of this song by Robert Burns, which is one of romantic love in which the poet tells his girlfriend he will meet her in the rye fields. Phoebe corrects Holden later on in the book. It should be 'If a body meet a body'.

Broadway was mobbed and messy The alliteration emphasizes the crowded, untidy thoroughfare.

Everybody Holden exaggerates, as he wants to give an idea of the crowds.

the Paramount, the Astor, the Strand, the Capitol All cinemas. A trip to the cinema was the universal entertainment of the Fifties.

millions of people . . . long, terrible lines The dreariness for waiting to get into the cinema is indicated.

the Lunts Alfred Lunt, the actor, married Lynn Fontanne and toured with her, playing leading parts in New York, Paris and Vienna.

Sir Laurence Olivier (1907–) The most distinguished and fascinating actor of his time.

The film of *Hamlet* Although much acclaimed in its day it now appears mannered and stilted, as Holden remarks.

Ophelia A character in *Hamlet*, the gentle, innocent girl who loves him.

the Mall A particularly wide path in Central Park which leads from the Zoo northward to the Lake.

Flys Up A game played with a soft ball.

that whole museum routine Holden has been to the museum so often as a primary school pupil that he remembers all the procedures associated with such visits.

Columbus, Ferdinand and Isabella Isabella of Castile (1451–1504) reigned jointly with her husband Ferdinand of Aragon over a united Spain from which Moors and Jews were expelled. During their reign they paid the expenses of Christopher Columbus, who sailed across the Atlantic and discovered the New World in 1492.

gasoline rainbows The colours that petrol makes in water.

Chapter 17

This chapter considers the relationship between men and women. It also continues the subject of phoneys. Holden regards the girls in the lobby sympathetically as being doomed to marry 'dopey guys'. He has little time for his own sex. He finds male conversation and habits uncongenial, though he does acknowledge that perhaps there is more to some people than might appear on the surface.

His reaction to Sally's arrival is a compound of admiration for her attractive appearance – and dislike verging on contempt for her loud voice and her gushing mannerisms. All through their date, these two emotions conflict. Holden is trying to assimilate the lovely Sally into his personal world, but failing disastrously. They are quite incompatible, but this is hard for Holden to accept. They have moments of physical pleasure, like the clinch in the taxi, but Sally's attitudes and utterances grate upon Holden.

Holden does not greatly enjoy the play; he is not satisfied with acting that is true to life. Indeed he says that the way the characters interrupted one another on stage was better than life-like, so it would appear that he is quarrelling with the fact that acting is an imitation of life. His writhing over the phoniness of the movie actor in the foyer and his dislike of the acquaintance Sally meets there is more understandable. As always, though, Holden is extreme. He talks of their revolting behaviour and reacts in a markedly hostile way to the entire conversation, which he imagines is aimed at excluding him. There is a certain amount of justification for Holden's attitude; Sally and George are theatrically exaggerating their reactions. His ill-temper is cooled, however, at Sally's suggestion that they go ice-skating, although he takes a perverse delight in noting how badly they both skate.

Holden's outburst illuminates some of the basic differences between himself and Sally, and also shows Holden's irrationality. Earlier in the book he decided to have nothing to do with girls he does not really like, yet here he asks Sally whom he despises to take part in his deepest dream. Sally represents all that Holden dislikes in social life. She enjoys the theatre, friends, decorating the Christmas tree. She wants to be seen skating in the attractive skirt, and is thoroughly conventional about graduation and marriage. He expresses his impotent fury at the urban social life he feels he is doomed to lead; much of what he criticizes is justified – the noise, the crowded streets, the rat-race of living. He mentions some of his unpleasant experiences during the past hours too, but Sally does not understand. To her, he seems incoherent.

He talks wildly about running away, leading an idyllic life in the backwoods with Sally, staying in log cabins and being self-sufficient. Escape is Holden's instinctive reaction to problems he can't solve. Sally cannot be expected to know or take this into consideration. She tries to calm him, to point out maturely that there will be time for such exploits after graduation. She complains because he is shouting in his excitement, and because she can't follow what he is trying to say.

Holden is now caught in the middle of the seesaw himself, between the childhood which he has turned from, and the adulthood which he despises, but towards which he is inexorably travelling. Small wonder that he sees flight as his only alternative. But Sally's pedestrian, prosy response to his invitation to join his private, idyllic world is understandably sufficient to bring all his barely concealed dislike of her to the fore, and he behaves for the only time in the book in a less than polite way. He swears at her.

Saturday Evening Post An illustrated family magazine.
I told you she'd go mad . . . the Lunts Holden speaks directly to the reader.
she was busy rubbering Sally was looking around to see who was there.
checkered vests Checked waistcoats.
Ivy League See note to Chapter 12.
slobbering around Holden's sour remark on the friendly way Sally greeted George.
Andover A prestigious college.
lulus A derogatory term. Fools.

fitting your pants . . . at Brooks' Having to have trousers made at the best tailor in town.

dirty little goddam clicks Cliques; exclusive groups which don't mix.

Massachusetts State in New England on the Atlantic Coast: capital, Boston. It is humid and hilly.

Vermont A state of New England near Canada.

Chapter 18

This chapter marks another pause in the action, during which several themes are pursued in preparation for the next encounter.

The author here views Holden and some of his ideas with an ironic eye. Holden ponders on the amazing differences between his assessments of people – which he is sure are always right – and those of girls who, in his opinion, can't tell conceit from inferiority complexes. Holden states that he hardly knew Al Pike, yet he calls him conceited because he spent his summer diving at the pool. Even clever girls, Holden muses, are unable to see people with clarity. Here Holden's snap judgements and immature prejudices, based on irrelevancies, are illustrated.

Jane Gallagher is to remain a memory, an unattainable dream throughout the book. Her purpose is to give Holden some ideal to strive for. So, although as always when he has suffered a disppointment, he thinks of her, he has to settle for a date with Carl Luce, who has already been mentioned as one of the people Holden considered telephoning immediately on his arrival in New York. Holden does not find inconsistent his wanting to spend an evening with someone he has twice said he doesn't like; but Carl is surprised at the call. Holden considers Carl, who is three years his senior, an intellectual.

Notice also that another character is prepared for here. Mr Antolini is mentioned for the first time, being one of the few names in Holden's address book. This glancing reference serves to point the reader's attention in readiness for the introduction of the character later on.

Another discussion on phoniness and the movies is introduced at this stage. The evening at Radio City is described in some detail, and for one who professes to scorn the movies as much as Holden does, it provides an opportunity for a good deal of adverse criticism. The film was preceded by a cabaret, very much in the style of the Fifties. Holden is unmoved by the

dancers' precision, depressed by thoughts of how much practising the roller-skater has had to do, and cynical about the
Christmas set-piece. He cannot relax and enjoy the entertainment because he is so concerned about its 'phoniness'.

He is far from being a 'sacrilegious atheist'. In fact, he takes
religion very seriously; defending it from mawkish sentimentality. He identifies Jesus' opinions with his own, and not
Sally Hayes' views. When he says the film was unbearably bad we
believe him; he recounts a predictable, clichéd plot in extraordinary detail and with every evidence of distaste. His caustic
comment on the character of the woman next to him, too
engrossed in this second-rate film to pay attention to her child,
shows his opinion of moviegoers.

The chapter ends with a digression on the army. Holden's
opinions are based on various comments and observations made
by D.B., who although in the army during the Second World
War, never experienced actual combat. D.B. disliked the army,
but not with the intensity of hatred felt by Holden who even
thinks it is phoney of D.B. to admire *A Farewell to Arms*, a book
about war. Holden ends the chapter emotionally – he'd rather
die, he says, than fight. This thinking was quite unfashionable
when the book was written, predating the refusal of many young
Americans to fight in the Vietnam war. It reveals again Holden's
independence of mind, as well as his overreaction to stimulus.

Fourth of July dance In celebration of American Independence Day.
Choate An American college.
half-gainer A type of dive.
Columbia An American University.
Charles Dickens See note to Chapter 1.
Oliver Twist A novel by Charles Dickens published in 1837. It is a
  fast-moving story of the London underworld and poverty.
come home on furlough On leave from the Army.
Rupert Brooke (1887–1915) A young poet of the 1914–18 war.
Emily Dickinson The greatest American woman poet. (1830–1886).
A Farewell to Arms Published in 1929 by Ernest Hemingway. It is the
  tragic story of an American soldier who falls in love with an English
  nurse in the 1914–1918 war.
Lieutenant Henry The hero of *A Farewell to Arms*.
Ring Lardner See note to Chapter 3.
The Great Gatsby A tragic story of love and betrayal by F. Scott
  Fitzgerald published in 1925.

Chapter 19

This chapter deals with the meeting between Holden and Luce, and Holden's receiving yet another rejection. He begins by describing in scathing, worldly wise tones the bar Luce had chosen for their meeting. He refers to it loftily as a place he had gradually stopped going to; he finds it depressing. The French cabaret singers are falsely cute, their songs are suggestive and sleazy, the barman is a snob and the clientele are phoney. Holden also describes them as flitty, which implies homosexuality. He finds this menacing, possibly because of his own sexual insecurity.

Although Luce has been described earlier to us as intelligent and intellectual, what absorbs Holden as he waits for their reunion is the role of sexual mentor that Luce has played to ignorant, gullible schoolboys in the past. This is a sphere about which Holden is becoming increasingly anxious after his recent experiences. While at school, Luce took a delight in describing sexual perversions, and in identifying those practised by public figures, for the benefit of his contemporaries.

Luce is blasé and selfassured, Holden appears a gauche schoolboy by comparison. The questions he asks Luce, all associated with sex, are immature. But he does not deserve the patronizing comments Luce makes. He remarks bitterly that Luce won't discuss serious matters with him. Luce, an older, more experienced boy, refuses to help when his advice is so clearly being sought. The cynical selfishness with which he ignores Holden's final plea for company is marked and unkind. Luce is offhand and cutting. He preserves his air of unapproachable maturity and refuses to communicate properly. He says that he finds Holden's pedantic insistence on morality and adherence to principle too naive to bear. Luce is still conscious of his image; asking the barman for drier drinks, dating a Chinese sculptress in her thirties, talking about the spiritual experience of sex. He impresses Holden with his world-weary air. It is noticeable that Holden does not remark on Luce's phoniness although to the reader that is his most striking quality.

The chapter finishes with a pointer to the end of the book. Luce laconically advises Holden to visit a psychiatrist. This gives us an external confirmation of Holden's predicament. Luce has had some psychiatric help himself, which is interesting for two reasons. It throws his self-confident character into perspective, and it also adjusts Holden to the idea that there is nothing sinister in psychiatry, since someone he admires has undergone it.

The meeting with Luce has been a failure. Their lack of communication confirms Holden's sense of isolation. Luce's refusal to stay condemns him to further loneliness.

Vooly Voo Fransay A phonetic rendering of the French 'Voulez-vous français' (Would you like French?). The title of a naughtily suggestive French song.

Connecticut A state in New England.

Flits Holden's word for homosexuals.

New Hampshire A state in New England bordering on Canada.

Is this ... Caulfield conversation Luce expresses weary indifference to Holden's opinions.

Nantucket In Massachusetts, the official end of the transatlantic sea crossing and a summer resort.

in the Village Greenwich village, arty suburb of New York. See note to Chapter 11.

chewed the fat Gossipped.

I have to tear He is in a hurry.

Chapter 20

Holden has now been rejected by everyone he has met. At the beginning of this chapter he works through his repertoire of reactions to difficult situations. He combines all the evasive techniques that he has used singly in other circumstances. This gives the reader a measure of the intensity of his feelings.

He makes eyes at the cabaret singer – just as he did at the three women in the Lavender Room. He sends an invitation to the singer to come and join him in a drink, just as he did at Ernie's. He drinks, even more heavily than he did at Ernie's. He pretends he has been shot, as he did after Maurice hit him. He wants to telephone Jane Gallagher, but can't bring himself to, just as when he first arrived at Penn Station, and again after the fight with Maurice. He telephones Sally Hayes instead, which is what he did after the fight with Maurice.

Holden is isolated, though Sally is remarkably pleasant to him after the way in which they had parted. The pianist whom he meets in the toilets, and the hatcheck girl, are both sympathetic but aloof. Holden's physical state reflects his mental one. He is still isolated, lonely and aimless. He feels unwanted, too, and tells the pianist he has no home. He is crying from depression.

By the time he breaks the record he bought for Phoebe he is at his lowest ebb. He is weak, shivering, his wet hair freezing. The Park is frightening; he feels he has nothing left. Even his present for Phoebe is shattered, like his life. It is hardly surprising that his mind turns morbidly to funerals, though his understanding of death is, like his understanding of love, still immature.

The image of Allie, lying alone in the cemetery in the rain while everyone else rushed for cover, is a poignant one. It illustrates clearly that Holden does not consider his brother dead at all, while at the same time showing his fear of death. When he throws away his remaining few coins, he has already decided to renounce the world. This puts his reckless spending of the last few days into perspective. He has been getting rid of his worldly possessions, in preparation for abandoning the life he finds so unfriendly.

The thought of his little sister Phoebe is the one force that can set him into motion. Once he has decided to go home, much of his paralysing depression lifts and he sees more clearly.

I . . . gave her the old eye Holden tried to flirt with her.
bullet in my guts Holden substitutes an imaginary physical hurt for his inward pain. Refer to Chapter 14.
Boy, was I blind He means he was drunk.
Trimma goddam tree for ya His drunken mind goes back to previous telephone conversations with Sally, when she insisted he should help decorate the Christmas tree.
Rocky's mob got me A gangster idiom from the films.
You oughta go . . . chap like you Holden is making a witty remark, though whether he realizes it or not is unclear.
Full of little hunks of ice Holden really did get very cold.
Detroit An industrial town in Michigan on the Great Lakes. It makes and exports Ford cars and planes.
Surrounded by . . . tombstones Holden's vision of death is a child-like one.
I sort of skipped . . . the nickel As one might skip pebbles, Holden rids himself of his remaining money; it seems so unimportant to him. There are 100 cents in a dollar; a quarter is 25 cents; a nickel is a five-cent piece.

Revision questions on Chapters 16–20

1 Describe the Museum of Natural History. What did Holden find so enjoyable about it?

2 There are several children described in Chapter 16. What are they doing? How does Holden treat them? In his conversation with the little girl, how does he speak to her?

3 Plays, actors and films are described on pages 123 (*Hamlet*), 131 and 132 (The Lunts) 144 and 145 (the film). What is Holden's attitude to them and to acting in general? Which did he dislike most and why?

4 After the ice-skating episode, why does Holden become so emotional? Go through his outburst and identify the things he takes exception to.

5 Write an extract from Sally Hayes's diary, describing her afternoon out with Holden – including the Lunts, the skating and their quarrel.

6 On pages 160–62 Holden muses on death and Allie. What leads him to such morbid thoughts?

7 Write up the meeting in Chapter 19 from Carl Luce's point of view.

8 On pages 146–7 Holden muses on war. Write down the facts he states.

9 On page 143 Holden reminisces about a Christmas show he saw. What is it that he finds so offensive? Add his remarks on Jesus to those he made previously.

10 Carl Luce, Stradlater and Ackley are all 2–3 years older than Holden. Now that you have met all three of them, can you see anything that they have in common, which would make Holden want to be friendly with them?

Chapter 21

This chapter and the next two show Holden at home, in the one environment in which he feels secure. His return is not without problems. He has the suspicious lift operator to fool, and once inside the apartment there are various obstacles. He compliments himself on his burglar-like technique. Details like the smell of home and the rattle of coathangers bring us to an appreciation of Holden's sense of belonging. He has to approach his sister's room carefully, and to search for her.

All the remarks he makes about her before he wakes her are approving and humorously relaxed. He is amused by her liking for D.B.'s big bed and desk; he admires her clothes and her neatness, he enjoys reading her notebooks. The contents of the notebooks are true to life, reflecting Phoebe's desire to adopt a more interesting middle name for herself, the work she is doing at school and the notes passed to classmates. They are innocent, straightforward and natural.

Phoebe is positive, energetic, enthusiastic and affectionate. She is delighted to see Holden. She puts her arms round him the moment she wakes, and won't let go of his hand. She is excited about her part in the school play and the film she has been to see that afternoon. She is anxious to communicate, and bubbling with information. In many ways she is similar to Holden himself, who earlier in the book recounted the plot of a film he saw. She rapidly conveys a great deal about herself, her relationship with her classmates and her family. Like Holden, she is emotional in her reactions, though his methods of expression are more restrained. She is vehement about her dislike of Curtis Weintraub and unrepentant about spoiling his jacket. At this point Holden assumes the adult, disapproving role for the first time in the book. The roles are soon reversed; when she realizes that Holden has been expelled from school she reacts extravagantly, magnifying parental attitudes. Holden knows that his parents are not going to kill him, but is still child enough to fear their disapproval. Phoebe is so disgusted with him that she will not speak to him for a time.

In the conversation with his sister Holden reveals a facet of his personality that is most pleasing. He is no longer in conflict or competition. He swears less; he relaxes to the point of not worrying about being caught. He can identify character traits in Phoebe that mirror his own, and knows how to deal with them. He speaks calmly when she is emotional, and knows when it is useless to struggle with her. Holden is more aware of her than of himself: his remark about her childish behaviour to Curtis Weintraub illuminates his attitude to Phoebe. He sees her as an equal, rather than as a child.

cough somewhere in Siberia Holden means that his mother is a light
  sleeper.
loafers Flat, moccasin-shaped shoes.
caning factories Phoebe's childish spelling of 'canning'.

Sagitarius . . . Taurus Two signs of the Zodiac. Phoebe misspells 'Sagittarius'.

Benedict Arnold (1741–1801) An American general in the War of Independence, and a traitor

Lister Foundation Joseph Lister, who inaugurated antiseptic surgery in 1865, set up this foundation supporting scientific research.

Kentucky An eastern central state in the Mississippi basin.

Annapolis A seaport, the capital of Maryland and location of the national World Academy.

a true madman One of Holden's recurring clichés, used here admiringly.

Colorado The highest state in America, in the Rocky Mountains. It is hardly likely there would be a ranch here.

Chapter 22

In this chapter Holden puts forward the central theme of the book, his concept of the Catcher in the Rye.

First, however, his isolation is re-emphasized. He mentions his ostracism by the fencing team and his father's lack of sympathy. The children agree that their father will not understand Holden. Phoebe, being younger, is more fearful but Holden has a tangible punishment in mind. He has been threatened with being sent to a military school. This would be an inappropriate environment for Holden, whose problems are not likely to be solved by discipline: and in fact the sanatorium he is sent to and the psychiatric treatment he receives at the end of the episode show that he has misjudged his parents' understanding.

Phoebe continues in the parental role, criticizing his frequent swearing and rapidly deflating Holden's notion of becoming a cowboy. She points out that he can't even ride. She is genuinely concerned about him, and Holden finds that she is the only person he can talk to who will listen to what he says.

He tries to express all the things that made Pencey so intolerable to him. What he does not realize is that it is life he is finding difficult, not only the school. He tells Phoebe about the cliques and pettinesses of people, and the phoney way in which inferiors have to defer to their superiors. He voices his dread of the ageing process, and the pointlessness and insignificance of most people's lives. But Holden cannot as yet generalize. He can only cite particular examples, which give his explanations a quality of incoherence because he is not fully aware of exactly what he finds so distasteful. This also gives his speech immediacy. He tells Phoebe about the Old Boy who searched for his initials on a toilet door while talking about how wonderful Pencey School was, and about Ackley's being banned from membership of a secret society. Even Mr Spencer, whom he liked, behaved phonily when the headmaster sat in his class.

As Phoebe says, Holden cannot think of very much that is pleasant or desirable: his mind is totally concentrated upon the negative. His vision has narrowed so much that he is left with his memories of Allie; James Castle who committed suicide in desperation rather than give in to social pressures; the nuns, and Phoebe herself. But only Phoebe is accessible to him; her importance to him is therefore paramount.

The timeless quality of myth is encapsulated in the figure of the Catcher in the Rye. Holden envisages himself as the protector of youth and innocence, guarding thoughtless children from falling over a cliff edge. The adult surrounded by children is benevolent but aloof. Symbolically, Holden has accurately portrayed himself as being part of the world of childhood but not belonging to it. It is a strange image, but a vivid one.

The real world is there, but no longer so menacing. Phoebe is prosaic and natural. Holden still has a last friend to turn to, one of his ex-teachers, Mr Antolini.

How's old Hazel Weatherfield Holden is trying to cajole Phoebe out of her bad mood by calling her by her pen-name.
a bull session Men talking together.
1776 The date of the start of the American War of Independence (known in the USA as 'the Revolution'). The thirteen original colonies secured their independence from Britain in 1783.
You don't like anything . . . happening Phoebe accurately points out Holden's depressive view of life.
too hot Too well.
turtleneck Crew-neck.
Robert Burns See note p.46 Chapter 16.
N.Y.U. New York University.

Chapter 23

Mr Antolini was mentioned in Chapter 18 as being one of the few people in Holden's address book. We are now given a little more information before Holden goes to Mr Antolini's apartment in the next chapter. Holden was particularly impressed that Mr Antolini picked up the body of James Castle. He also feels that he can speak freely to him, and says immediately that he has been expelled. Mr Antolini invites Holden over, though it is very late and he had already gone to bed.

Holden seems to be subconsciously courting detection. He does not want to leave, and dances with Phoebe; he is relaxed and beginning to enjoy himself. He knows the maid is in the house and could have heard the music. When their parents return they see the light, and his mother smells the cigarette smoke. As Holden says at the end of the chapter, it would have been an easy way out if he had been caught at that point. We are aware of his physical tiredness as well as his depressed state.

The visit home and seeing Phoebe again affects Holden more than he had realized. He is overwrought, and cries when he has to leave. He is bearing a burden much too heavy, and has found nobody except Phoebe to confide in.

We catch our only glimpse of Holden's mother in this chapter. So far we have been told that she is still depressed over Allie's death, and that she will be upset to hear of Holden's expulsion. She is firm but kind to Phoebe; there is no discernible reason why Holden should hide from her.

Phoebe is quick-witted: she lies without hesitation about the cigarette. She is generous: she offers Holden her Christmas shopping money. She very loving and intuitive: she doesn't want Holden to go away; her voice sounded strange when she said he wouldn't see her in the play at school, because she has realized he fully intends to go to California.

As an echo to his leaving Pencey, another secure environment, Holden again sneaks out of a building at night by the stairs, and falls over. This parallels the two episodes, pointing their similarities. Both Pencey and home were places where he was established in a community, and had people to talk to. He left both places of his own free will. The ending rounds off the three chapters, with the reference to the liftboy who was duped at the beginning of the episode.

snappy Quick.
Yogi guys People who practise Yoga.
corny dips Stylised gliding and downward movements in ballroom dancing.
young lady Phoebe's mother is being formal to show she is annoyed.
Her voice sounded funny Holden realizes Phoebe is upset.
stop on a goddam dime Once you start crying it's difficult to stop.

hunting hat . . . to her See Notes on symbolism (p.85).

Chapter 24

The progress of Holden's illness is mentioned more frequently from now on to the end of the book. Holden has reached the stage where his mental turmoil, combined with his lack of food and sleep and the bitter cold are having a marked effect upon him. He remarks in passing that he felt dizzy when he got outside, and took a cab rather than walk the moderate distance from his home to the Antolinis'. He mentions that he felt dizzy and had a headache when Mr Antolini was talking to him. His tiredness is stressed several times, and he is finally overcome, yawns and has to sleep.

Mr Antolini, though not appearing until late in the book, has been friendly with Holden and his family for some time. He took an interest in Holden when they were both at Elkton Hills school, is in touch with D.B. and dined with Mr Caulfield only two weeks previously. He is witty, and uses some of the same over-dramatized speech forms as Holden himself. He exaggerates Holden's height, and refers to the melodramatic way in which Holden had spoken on the telephone. He is often ironic – which Holden resents occasionally. He is a clever man as well as a perceptive one. The advice he gives Holden is excellent. He realizes that Holden is under stress but doesn't comprehend the full depth of his nervous exhaustion.

Mrs Antolini is briefly sketched, but only as essential background. It is important that Mr Antolini is seen to have a wife with whom he is on good terms, so that the encounter at the end of the chapter remains ambiguous. We are told by Holden that she is serious, an intellectual, older than Mr Antolini and rich. He mentions that she played tennis. She had got out of bed to prepare coffee for them, and returns there rapidly. She says little, but seems friendly. Holden, who is impressed by physical beauty, is taken aback at her unattractive appearance.

One of the subjects discussed in this chapter is literary style; digression in particular. Holden acknowledges that he likes digressions. He relishes it when others digress, because then, he says, he can be sure that people are discussing something that really interests them. He acknowledges that this is the style he adopts, as is of course evident in the book, because he prefers an unstructured approach. When considered in this light, it is clear that *The Catcher in the Rye*, using what is called the 'stream of consciousness' technique (see p.7), is more complex than it appears. All Holden's memories of people and places have had to be incorporated into the narrative, and this accounts for the occasional hesitancies and changes of subject within chapters.

There are similarities between the interview with Mr Spencer and that with Mr Antolini. Both are Holden's teachers who like him and have his interests in mind. They both try to communicate and advise Holden. In both cases he goes willingly to their homes, and meets their wives.

Mr Antolini tries to warn Holden that his attitude to life is wrong, and that he will come to a bad end if he does not participate more, and take an interest in his studies. He over-dramatizes the situation, but his intention is good. Mr Antolini makes the same mistake as Mr Spencer, in trying to fit Holden into a social mould that he has outgrown. Holden is not confused or sickened by human behaviour; he is wearied by its phoniness. He has seen through many of the conventions of society that still bind the Mr Spencers and Mr Antolinis. He has no interest in making his way in society. So Mr Antolini's remark about dying nobly for a cause, and the quotation he gives Holden are both inappropriate. Holden is not interested in causes or material success. He wants peace.

The way in which Holden reacts to Mr Antolini's speech is reminiscent of his behaviour in Mr Spencer's room. He focuses on Mr Antolini's drinking, and makes disparaging remarks to himself about how drunk the man is. He interrupts him to make minute corrections, like the exact name of Mr Vinson. He agrees with what Mr Antolini is saying much too readily, just as he did with Mr Spencer. And Mr Antolini too feels that Holden is not completely on the same wavelength; he writes down the quotation to make sure that Holden will read it. Holden as before manages to maintain a polite facade while inwardly thinking of other things.

The importance of the incident in the night lies in Holden's interpretation of Mr Antolini's caressing his head rather than in Mr Antolini's motives. The scene is left deliberately ambiguous. It is debatable that Mr Antolini was half-drunkenly allowing submerged homosexualism to surface. He didn't actually do anything apart from patting Holden's head; an innocent enough gesture in itself.

Throughout the book Holden's fear of any sexual activity has been constantly stressed. He is physically repelled by anything homosexual; saying he doesn't even like to talk about this, such is his distaste. This is one area he cannot cope with. It is not surprising that he ran.

Forest Hills See note on Chapter 15.
Long Island Part of New York City, separated from the mainland by the East River. It contains Queens and Brooklyn, boroughs of New York City. Some areas are holiday resorts.
highball Whisky and soda with ice, served in a tall glass.
just dandy Absolutely fine (slang more of the Thirties than of the Fifties).
a little oiled up He has had a few drinks.
Buffalo Port on Lake Erie, in New York state.
in short order Rapidly.
brace A support to strengthen the leg wasted by polio.
peek Peep.
I know it. I know he is Compare some of the things Holden says to Mr Spencer on pages 13 and 15.
Wilhelm Steckel (1868–1940) A psychoanalyst, friend of Jung and Freud. Very interested in maturation processes. The quotation implies that it is a mark of maturity to be able to live with oneself.
dress your mind An extended metaphor, in which Mr Antolini compares the mind to a figure that has to be clothed in appropriate garments.

Chapter 25

We are now made very aware of Holden's illness as he reaches the crisis in his conflict. He feels feverish, his eyes hurt, he has a headache and sores in his mouth. He can't eat, yet he wants to vomit. He has diarrhoea and faints in the toilet. He also has the sensation, noticed first when he crossed the road to Mr Spencer's house, that he is disappearing whenever he steps off the kerb. Now, however, the feeling is so intense that he has to call upon Allie for help.

His physical state is a reflection of his mental turmoil. He finds himself wondering if he was right in running so hastily from Mr Antolini's house. His seasonal surroundings if anything intensify his depression. He is aware of the tawdriness of the Santa Clauses and the girls without makeup; and he notices the incongruity of the men swearing as they unload a Christmas tree. The children in the streets remind him of other, happier Christmases with Phoebe. This has the effect of improving his spirits. Phoebe is the only person whom he wishes to see again. He plans a farewell.

Holden extends the idea he first expounded to Sally Hayes at the skating rink, that of retreating from life to a cabin. Because all the times he has tried to communicate with others have proved failures, he has the idea of living as a deaf-mute, and communicating by note-writing. The idea is extreme, and Holden's vision of marriage to a beautiful deaf-mute is absurd, but it does have its logic in view of his recent experiences. He begins, appropriately, by writing a note to Phoebe asking her to meet him at the museum. The cabin will be a place where no one is allowed to behave phonily. This is the most important rule. It will be open to his family.

When, in search of Phoebe, Holden revisits the primary school he used to attend he is made aware that it is he who has changed. The school is timeless. He notices the details that were the same when he was there. The stillness of a school in lesson time makes him feel even more isolated and lonely. He is outraged to see the graffiti on the wall, particularly because he has so recently identified himself with the Catcher in the Rye, protector of innocence. He feels that in a school of all places children should be free from taint. He tries to rub it out, but when he sees another obscenity on a wall in the museum he begins to realize that one person is incapable of preventing corruption. He is also aware, in the tomb in the museum, where he had hoped to find peace, that no place is free from the taint of the vulgar; not even his own gravestone. He is therefore now subconsciously aware that there is no escape from the world. The two little boys, who are evidently playing truant from school, amuse Holden for a while.

The arrival of Phoebe with the suitcase sparks off the resolution of his inner conflict. When he realizes her plan to accompany him he knows he can no longer run away. He cannot take her with him and his affection for her is too great to allow him to turn his back on her. He also sees in her childish, burdened arrival a reflection of his own immature behaviour. Phoebe turns the tables on Holden by reacting to his nastiness with dogged stubbornness. She refuses to return to school, and is more determined than Holden ever manages to be. This worries him because he knows he can't control her when she is in this mood.

The final scene is very visual. Phoebe is on the roundabout

while Holden watches her, getting soaked in the rain. But his mind is at rest. He has resolved to go home and return the responsibility for his life to his parents; he has found it too much to bear. It is an idyllic picture, because of the contentment that radiates from the two of them. Holden is almost crying with happiness; his love for Phoebe is evident in the way he watches her. The image of life as a roundabout, or a circle, is a trite one, but Holden has tried to direct his life along more ambitious paths and failed. He is only sixteen. He needs a period of calm and predictability which is symbolized by the carousel.

Bloomingdale's A New York department store.
way up in the Sixties Streets to the North of the commercial area near Central Park.
Holland Tunnel Two vast twin tunnels for cars under the Hudson, joining Manhattan Island to the mainland at Jersey City.
bum a ride Hitch-hike.
somebody's just taken a leak The stairs smelt of urine.
carousel Roundabout.
grab for the gold ring In the centre of the roundabout.

Chapter 26

This is a short note at the end of the book. The reader is made aware that Holden is now getting proper treatment, and that his stay in the rest home is only temporary. He is going back to school in the autumn. He makes no promises to do better than before in his studies, but there is a little hope. Holden does not hate anybody; he misses even the people who treated him unfairly. He does not indulge in recriminations but lives for the present.

This short chapter rounds the book off structurally and in time, by referring to Holden's present whereabouts, and the visits of D.B., which were briefly alluded to in Chapter 1. But we are left with no conclusion as such. Life is not something that rounds itself off, or ties up the loose ends. We are given no further information about any of the characters we have met. This gives the book the effect of truth. It is as though our conversation with Holden Caulfield is now at an end.

Revision questions on Chapters 21–26

1 Write down the things that particularly appeal to you about Phoebe.

2 In some ways Phoebe is still very childish. Write a list of these, including her clothes, her habits, her interests.

3 Now write a list of the ways in which she seems more adult than her years. Remember she is only ten.

4 How does Holden try to tell Phoebe the things he dislikes about school? Discuss what he says about the Old Boy, Mr Spencer and James Castle.

5 These people are also involved in Holden's concept of phoniness. What do these chapters add to our understanding of phoniness?

6 Write an account of that evening as Phoebe would have told it to her best friend.

7 Using the information on pages 193–97, explain exactly what Mr Antolini is trying to say to Holden.

8 Describe Holden's visit to his primary school.

9 Describe Phoebe's behaviour at the zoo. Trace how she gradually forgave Holden, from the sea lions to the bears and the carousel.

10 What do you think of the end of the book? Does it satisfy you? Do you wish Salinger had finished it off more precisely? What are the things you would like to know?

11 Write an alternative ending.

Salinger's art in *The Catcher in the Rye*
The characters

Holden Caulfield

A teenage idealist who becomes submerged in the seamy side of adult society and almost succumbs.

From Holden's own account of his adventures, and to a lesser extent from what we can observe of his speech and actions, and the reactions of others to him, we learn about his character. He is like all teenagers, a mixture of moods and attitudes, searching for secure values. He is trying to establish his own personality in a world of conflicting attitudes in which he feels there is no guidance. It is this lack of positive structure to his life that is most tellingly modern. He is intelligently aware of the choices available, but appears to have received no formal instruction on religious, moral or social values.

  He is virtuous: it is his very goodness and open-ness that lead him into difficulties. He expects others to be like himself. He is sympathetic and thoughtful – he appreciates the tedium of the bellboy's job, asks Ackley out in spite of his dislike of him and visits Mr Spencer because he has the flu. He is interested in individuals, not the system. He feels sorry for Sunny the prostitute. He notices details such as her green dress and the pearl-grey hat the little boy's father was wearing. He remarks on Mrs Morrow's rings and magazine, and the nun's cheap spectacles. He appreciates the vulnerability of nuns and children, but finds himself alone in his responses. Holden is an idealist in a materialistic society. He finds that his high ideals, such as honesty (which he expresses as lack of phoniness) and consistency are not achieved by the adult world he soon must join, and he becomes steadily more depressed.

  Society ignores the weak, applauding showmanship and fraud. Holden hates hypocrites, or phoneys, but meets few people who are honest. To his consternation everyone around him is involved. Even his teachers are phoneys; Mr Spencer toadies to the head, headmasters pander to rich parents, and Mr Antolini proves to have suspect morals. The night-clubs he visits are full of phoneys; Sally Hayes adores them and is one herself. The acclaimed Lunts and Olivier, Ernie and the cabaret singers are praised by all except Holden; even his brother D.B. has gone to Hollywood, the phoniest place of all. The books Holden likes are those which speak to him as to a friend, and use colloquial idioms and a digressive style. He thinks of Jesus as a contemporary and considers what he would do in various circumstances. The few people who are not phonies are either dead like Allie and James Castle, beyond his reach like Jane Gallagher, or outside the world like the nuns and children. War he sees as the greatest phoniness of all.

Although Holden is innocent he is not naive. Society has tarnished him to the extent that he is aware of the cost of things. He refers to the value of his coat, his cases, his typewriter, even his pens. He does not cherish possessions. They do not interest him. His coat and gloves were stolen, and he only regrets the cold; he felt like swapping his expensive cases with Dick Slagle; he gives the nuns far more than he can afford. He is as anti-materialistic as it is possible to be while living in society. As a child he lost his belongings – now as an adolescent he fails to pick up his change, despises people who frequent swanky restaurants and popular bars; yet there is that inconsistent element in him which makes him take taxis, go to bars, cinemas and theatres, and stay in hotels. It is this acquiescent part of him he is rejecting when he tries to divest himself of all he owns and throws his last few coins into the lake.

Sex fascinates and repels Holden at the same time; he longs to find out what it is all about, to experience that passion hinted at by Stradlater and envied by Ackley. He has already established that monasticism is not for him: he enjoys women's company and looks forward to a full sexual life. He watches voyeuristically from his hotel window but finds the physical reality unappealing; Sunny's efforts to arouse him he considers dirty; Mr Antolini's touch on his head causes flight. Sex, so prized by the adult world, he finds worthless. He admits that he doesn't know what it is all about. Jane Gallagher fulfils his romantic, idealistic soul.

Holden is aware of the importance of social standing – he knows that he and Sally are more likely to get on because their families are so similar; he can't share a room with someone who is insecure about status. The boys he mentions are in the 'Ivy League' universities, or go to prep schools. This appreciation of status can be linked with his behaviour. He seems anxious to keep up with his contemporaries, behaving in a calculatedly extrovert way with Stradlater, hurling insults at him after his date with Jane, tap-dancing in the toilet, playing in the snow as though inviting recognition, and being rude to Ackley, refusing to answer his questions and tormenting him by pretending to be blind. He talks cynically of Ossenburger's visit to the school. His friends find him immature: this is hardly surprising since they are two years older. Ackley and Luce both tell him to grow up; Stradlater displays a great deal of patience before knocking him down. He agrees too readily with his teachers, as though he doesn't want to communicate completely with them.

Society robs Holden of everything; of both his brothers and his parents' presence; Stradlater borrows all he has, his clothes, his mind and even his girl. Maurice cheats him. His possessions are stolen at school, Dick Slagle appropriates his cases while criticizing his pens. The tangible expression of his grief at Allie's death, the mitt, is spurned by the insensitive Stradlater. It is hardly surprising that he eventually rejects society, when he expresses his impotent rage in the tirade at the skating rink. Small wonder then that he feels it is to children he must turn. The vivid motif of the Catcher in the Rye epitomizes the only future Holden can see for himself. Phoebe is the only touchstone left to him. The thought of her naturalness, her sanity restores Holden to confidence in life. His love for her prevents him from a complete breakdown by the pond in the Park, and from a wild, pointless escape later.

It is hardly surprising that Holden feels isolated. He is a loner. Everyone in whom he confides rejects him; few even bother to try and understand what motivates him. When he stands up for his rights he is knocked down. He considers himself a coward because he is not a bully. People don't listen to what he says; he spends a good deal of time thinking about telephoning people; he awakens people to talk to them, but all except Phoebe reject him. Even when he does talk, there is no real understanding. Horwitz talks about fish instead of ducks; Antolini misinterprets his reasons for dropping out of school. The isolation reaches its height in the desolate scene by the lake, and is continued in the womb-like stillness of the museum. Holden is more at ease when the burden of efforts at communication have been removed from him.

He questions life constantly, trying to make sense of its

contradictions. Allie's death made him react at first with uncharacteristic violence, then in images of rare imagination. The ducks, the hunting hat and the Catcher show a personality of strength and sensitivity. His disgust at the word on the wall and his eventual realization that people, even his own sister, cannot be forever protected but must face the hazards of life, enable Holden to reach a precarious equilibrium.

Perhaps the most touching of Holden's characteristics is that although he comes perilously close to breaking, seeing himself isolated, friendless and autistic, he never shows bitterness. His essential goodness is not harmed. Human behaviour saddens but does not anger him. The movies which he professes to hate give him a means of transmuting inward pain into the physical, by miming scenes of gunfights. In many ways he exhibits the essence of Christianity which he struggles to express in his certainty that Jesus would never have hated anyone enough to send them to hell.

Mr Spencer

Mr Spencer is an ageing teacher, although not as old or decrepit as Holden imagines, who is genuinely fond of his students. He and his wife regularly invite boys over to their house and treat them informally. Holden is almost like a son in their home. He is certain of their affection, and he likes Mr Spencer enough to apologize for his poor History paper. Mr Spencer finds pleasure in small things, like buying the Navajo blanket. His strident voice and pedantic speech annoy Holden who does not like Mr Spencer's habit of calling him 'boy'. He uses outmoded idioms, repeats himself, and laughs at his own jokes. Holden is repelled by Mr Spencer's body, as he cannot come to terms with physical decay or illness, but Mr Spencer seems unaware of this. He is not worried that he twice fails to hit the bed with papers. He senses that he is not in total communication with Holden, but fails to understand why. In some ways Mr Spencer is quite childlike; he picks his nose while Holden is watching; he talks of life being a game. Apart from deferring in what Holden sees as a phoney way to the headmaster, he is sincere and Holden respects him. In his attempt to bring home the seriousness of Holden's failure, he is unpleasantly sarcastic, detailing the number of schools that have expelled Holden and reading out his exam paper. Holden and he uphold different sets of values; the teacher is on the side of the establishment, Holden interested in the individual and integrity at all costs; that is why they cannot communicate.

Robert Ackley

Ackley is an insensitive teenager who does not know how to make friends. Nobody even likes him enough to give him a nickname. He is cordially disliked by most of the other boys who will not let him join their secret fraternity. He rarely goes out, even to the big match on that first afternoon, and has no social life. He is not fond of Mal Brossard, and is both jealous of and curious about Stradlater's success with girls. He fantasizes about sexual adventures although Holden is sure he is a virgin.

Holden remarks on his social ineptitude. He touches Stradlater's and Holden's belongings, sits on the arms of the chairs, and cleans his fingernails in Holden's room. His behaviour is immature; he laughs when the tennis racquet falls on Holden's head. He is insensitive: asking Holden if his parents are aware of his expulsion and commenting loudly on the loss of the fencing foils. He is grudging about Howie Coyle's prowess at basketball, saying it is all due to his build. He fails to notice Holden's many hints that he is unwanted. He regards Holden as immature and takes little notice of what he says. His physical cleanliness is minimal; both Stradlater and Holden comment on his teeth, and he does not often change his socks. His room smells. He snores and has bad breath. The only person he can relate to appears to be Holden, who does not like him constantly coming unannounced into his room.

Ackley is aware to a certain extent of his deficiencies; when Holden visits his room after the fight his face is covered in spot cream. Although he is gauche, he is patient on being awakened by Holden. He is concerned over the bleeding. He is steadfast about his religion, and high-principled enough to refuse Holden permission to sleep in his absent room-mate's bed. As Holden says, Ackley has so many problems that in the end one can only feel sorry for him.

Ward Stradlater

He is handsome and conscious of his own good looks. Holden remarks acidly that he spends a great deal of time looking in mirrors, and that he is accustomed to being waited on because he is so attractive in spite of his lack of hygiene. Holden is particularly disgusted by Stradlater's filthy razor. He is sexually experienced and seductive according to Holden, who becomes extremely apprehensive about Jane's date with him. Ackley is more openly jealous of him than Holden; he leaves the room when Stradlater appears, and tells Holden that Stradlater is conceited. It is apparent, however, that Holden is also jealous from the aggressive way he behaves towards him in the toilets. When Stradlater appears he is energetic, purposeful, too self-centred to quarrel with the boys. He selfishly borrows Holden's jacket, hair-cream, and commandeers his time to write an essay.

On his return from the date, Stradlater's insensitivity is apparent. He is unaware of Holden's inner turmoil, until Holden tears up the essay and attacks him. He is unimaginative, disliking the essay because it is not on a conventional subject. He thinks that English is a matter of punctuation. Stradlater's self-absorption which extended to indifference over Holden's tap-dancing antics in the toilets becomes less pleasing as he shows his impatience at Jane's only signing out for 9.30 on her date with him. He seems arrogant and narcissistic. He initially remains calm when Holden attacks him, disregarding his puny blows in the knowledge that his superior strength will win. However, gradually and understandably Stradlater loses patience when Holden becomes more abusive. No one can blame him for his final treatment of Holden; he showed forbearance and even concern to the last.

Phoebe Caulfield

Phoebe is a link with Holden's own childhood. She rollerskates in the park, preferring the same areas he did, attends the same primary school, writes notes to her friends in her books and visits the museum. He is proud of her, encourages and relishes the childishness in her, like miming the action of the film, because this keeps time at bay. He is surprised when he considers that she is already ten; not a small child any longer. She is a potent force for good: it is his love for her which rescues him from suicide and it is his realization that she is growing up and must be allowed to reach for the gold ring that changes his self-destructive spiral and allows him to go home.

Although a strong symbol, Phoebe is consistently portrayed as natural, often down-to earth, as when she pours cold water on his idea of becoming a cowboy by telling him he can't even ride, taking belching lessons and peeling off a piece of sticking plaster to reveal her cut. She is childishly serious about her dancing, and the idea of controlling her temperature. Her exaggeration is childlike too, for instance, her reaction to Holden's expulsion when she repeats incessantly her fear that her father will kill him. She dramatizes many of her feelings, turning her back on Holden, not speaking to him at night and again the next day when they quarrel. She is demonstrative in her affections, holds hands with her brother, insists on accompanying him in his flight and carefully keeps the broken pieces of the record.

Like Holden she has marked enthusiasms; she recounts the plot of the film she has seen, loves writing and is passionate about her part in the school play and the behaviour of her friend's mother at the cinema. Holden says she is clever, and she is certainly astute; deceiving her mother, reading Holden's expression when he intends leaving her for good, asking him about his future in an adult way, and diagnosing the negativism of which he has so far been unaware.

Holden says that she is the one person whose judgement he can trust: she is quick to perceive phoniness in films and people. He often wishes he had her to talk to when he is feeling lonely and miserable. Although there are sentimental overtones at the end of the novel as Holden stands by the roundabout in the rain, Phoebe is credibly drawn.

Sally Hayes

Sally is very attractive, and enjoys being admired. The Hayes and Caulfield families have known one another a long time and are on the same social level. This is one reason Holden goes out with her. As he explains in the parable about the suitcases, he thinks it important to stay within one's own class. She is a socialite; impressed by boys who attend the prestigious universities, and she boasts to Holden about their asking her out. She is impressed by the names of well-known actors like the Lunts, and incapable of distinguishing the good from the second-rate. She enjoys the cabaret show that Holden finds offensive because of its hackneyed sentimentalism. She wants to go skating not because she can skate but because she can hire a skirt. Although Holden hates to admit it, she is a phoney. He says her letter inviting him over to decorate the tree is phoney and when he phones her she pretends that she does not recognize his voice.

When Holden tries to communicate his thoughts to her at the rink her sense of convention is affronted. She has a narrow, tunnel vision, and cannot envisage Holden's dissatisfaction with the life she finds so pleasant. Nor can she imagine following any other than a conventional lifestyle.

She sets up a conflict within Holden because physically he desires her, but on all other levels he despises her.

Carl Luce

Luce is an arrogant poseur, included in the book to place Holden again in context as an immature sixteen-year-old, to provide him with another rejection and also, strangely, to point the way to a psychiatric cure.

Fascinated by sex in his adolescence, and enjoying the power of enlightening younger boys about its perversions, he is an object of attraction to Holden although he doesn't like him and resists telephoning him until he has tried everyone else. When asked for advice, Luce is patronizing about Holden's ignorance, rejecting Holden's moral code as childish. He doesn't take the time to examine Holden's approach – he is certain that his own is the only one. He enjoys boasting about his sophisticated life-style, Chinese mistress and new-found interest in Oriental philosophy. Holden is accustomed to his laconic attitude, and surprisingly does not comment on his phoniness although that is marked, but bitter that his questions are unanswered. Luce is clever but unsympathetic and self-centred.

Mr Antolini

Mr Antolini is a pleasant, relaxed figure, genuinely fond of Holden. Consequently his betrayal of Holden is cataclysmic, resulting in almost complete mental turmoil.

Although it is the middle of the night and he and his wife are tired and in bed after a party, they get up to welcome and talk to him. His action in picking up the dead James Castle, not caring about his jacket, identifies him with the forces of good in the book. He has an agreeably humorous attitude to Holden, although Holden finds his wit oppressive at times. There are indications in the dialogue that Mr Antolini is a little over-intimate in his manner when he compliments Holden on his composition-writing for instance, and when he remarks on his good looks, but he also adopts an intellectual approach; when they are talking about digressions for example, or when he is explaining to Holden that he is going to face a difficult future without an education. His excessive drinking can be viewed in two ways; he might be drinking to cover embarrassment and concealed homosexual desires while talking to Holden, or he is genuinely rather drunk. If his advice is to be viewed as serious, though irrelevant to Holden, then his stroking Holden's hair in the night might well suggest homosexuality. If he was drunk then neither his advice nor his later behaviour can be taken seriously. The scene is ambiguous: the reader must decide if Mr Antolini is nursing homosexual tendencies or cherishing a paternal wish for a son he will never have.

Minor characters

Mrs Morrow
Holden meets her in the train when he leaves Pencey. She is the mother of one of the boys there.

Mrs Morrow appears when Holden needs support. She represents female attraction without challenging Holden's sexuality. Holden can safely flirt with her; she is gentle, motherly in the nicest sense, and in public, on a train. This contrasts with Stradlater's encounters in the dark of Ed Banks' car. Mrs Morrow is desirable; although forty-five, she is good-looking, richly ornamented with rings and an orchid. Her voice and smile are pleasant, her manner charming and soothing to Holden's nerves. She is susceptible, it seems, to Holden's flattery about her son. She suffices to make Holden feel he is again on the ascendant since she seems so easy to deceive. She provides him with reassurance about his manhood and appeal.

Faith Cavendish
Holden was given her telephone number at a party by an acquaintance. He thinks she is a stripper and hopes she will come to his room.

Faith Cavendish is produced as yet another rejection for Holden, the second in the hurtful trio of females who prove to him that he is not as mature as he thought. She is interesting for her abrupt changes in manner as various key signals are given to her. She begins nastily, in what one assumes is her true voice. Holden refers to her feline attributes. She screams at him for waking her up and leaves off the ends of her words in an echo of a common accent. The first key-word is Princeton, a prestigious university. At the mention of its name, she immediately becomes ladylike, frosty but no longer vulgar. She manages to combine suspicion of Holden with awe at the university. We are left with the impression that she would have met him if Holden had been less pressing, and if he had not mentioned the second key-word, phone-booth. This does not impress her. Although she makes her excuses, this is not a total rejection.

Sunny

She is the prostitute sent to Holden's hotel room by the bullying pimp of a lift-boy. Through her Holden realizes he is not interested in sex without love.

Sunny is businesslike, common and bored. Her greeting is offhand; unused to being considered as a person she is amazed that Holden wants to talk to her. Her voice is thin. Holden finds her quite unnerving. She lacks interest in life – her main concern seems to be in taking care of her dress. She is not deceived by Holden's false name or age, nor by his declaration of a recent operation. It seems that she is piqued by his rejection of her. She is astute enough to realize that he does not find her alluring: hence her spiteful return with Maurice to extort money. Holden finds her attempts to arouse him offensive. Through her he loses face, but also learns that sex without love is worthless. In fact, Holden's encounter with her strengthens his idealism.

The nuns

Holden meets them in the station where he breakfasts after his encounter with Sunny and Maurice.

Like Mrs Morrow, they appear when Holden needs them most. They are not clearly differentiated, though the one with the glasses and the kind smile does most of the talking. Not only do they represent innocent womanhood after the sleazy deviousness of Sunny, they provide a contrast with all the social, veneered mothers Holden knows. They are a touchstone he cherishes, two of the few totally non-phoney people he meets.

Mrs Caulfield

Holden's mother who is often referred to but only glimpsed once through the door of a cupboard.

It would have been too simplistic for the author to represent Holden's mother as overtly rejectful, so we are allowed only fragmentary knowledge of her. Never does Holden refer to her less than affectionately, yet never does he state a wish to return to her: it is always Phoebe who represents security. We are told that she still grieves over Allie, and can become quite hysterical. That is the reason for Holden's not returning home in the first place. Other snippets confirm this; when Holden was a child she would be cross if he lost possessions. She made scenes about the Gallaghers' dog, and then felt snubbed when Mrs Gallagher cut her in town. She won't allow the radio to be played in traffic for fear it should distract the driver. She sends him hockey instead of racing skates, and Holden pictures her worrying what to do with his sports equipment if he dies. She knows intuitively, according to Holden, if one of her children is on the phone and wakes up if she hears him, yet when he is actually in Phoebe's room she does not sense his presence.

What we hear of her conversation with Phoebe through the cupboard door displays her maternal concern. She worries over Phoebe's language, asks about her trip out with a friend and scolds her for smoking a cigarette.

Allie Caulfield

Holden's intelligent, guileless younger brother who had died of leukaemia aged eleven, three years previously.

The character of Allie has two functions which counter-balance one another. His tragic death explains much of Holden's depression and loneliness. It explains Holden's lassitude and lack of ambition in life. On the other hand his continuing presence in Holden's thoughts is a substitute for religion. Holden talks to him at times of severe stress; after Maurice beats him up, and at the end of the book when he feels he is disappearing. Without Allie to support him Holden would have given up.

Allie was intelligent – teachers loved him; he was sensitive and contemplative, writing poems on his fielding mitt, had a strong sense of humour, and a friendly nature that was never angry. Holden cannot forget him.

Jane Gallagher

Jane is a shadowy character, seen through Holden's recollections of a holiday two years previously. She rapidly becomes a symbol of innocent girlhood and romantic love in its most idealized form.

Jane aroused Holden's protective instincts against her step-father on that summer holiday. These resurface, and his feelings of sexual inadequacy rapidly turn into anger and jealousy against Stradlater for going out with her. The girl herself is portrayed as an unchanging innocent, victim of man's desires. Holden whose love is pure cannot risk allowing his own sexual feelings about her to emerge; if he does he too would join the ranks of the booze-hound with undertones of incest, and the sensual Stradlater whom he views as a rapist. He thinks of telephoning her many times, and indeed does so twice, but fails to speak to her. Jane is sketched in as being fond of sport, ballet, interested in poetry, sensitive and reticent. She never divulges why she rubs a tear into the checker board, nor does she repeat the stroking of Holden's neck that he finds so seductive. She can be seen as a symbol of Holden's fear of the loss of childhood.

Much has been made of her failure to move her kings from the back row. It can be viewed as showing her fear of sex, and indeed it is a virginal, unattainable gesture on her part as is her signing out for 9.30 on a Saturday night. Even Cinderella stayed out later than Jane Gallagher.

Themes

Background and timesetting

The Catcher in the Rye was first published in 1951, arousing considerable controversy. It emphasized personal judgement, daring to counter establishment values such as loyalty to school, social stability and middle-class consumerism. Because of this and its frank language, it was banned in various countries: in San Jose (USA), in Australia (1957) and South Africa (1958). American teachers were suspended for issuing the book, but it has always been popular with the young. Ian Ousby (see *Further reading*) points out that it was linked with the 1950s rebellious movement of *Lucky Jim* (Kingsley Amis) and *Look Back in Anger* (John Osborne) and became a cult among teenagers who saw themselves mirrored there. Lawrence Lipton in *The Holy Barbarians* notes that it exerted a great influence on the Beat Generation, and it was published in the same year as Kerouac's *On The Road*, another cult book.

Post-war British society confronted this representative of a nation conspicuous for self-indulgent extravagance and social pretension. Although Holden's predicament was intriguing, he could not at the time be taken completely seriously by the majority of young readers, few of whom had much to do with hotels, restaurants or bars. Now that British social style has moved in the direction of America, the book seems even more relevant than it did thirty-five years ago.

Money

Do Holden's problems stem from being over-indulged? Could his reckless spending be because he hates his mother? She was furious when he lost things as a child, and now he seems to take a delight in losing or having things stolen. Mothers are pictured in swanky restaurants, as opposed to nuns, whom Holden admires.

Holden moves in wealthy circles; he remarks that the Spencers have to open the door themselves because they don't have a maid. Pencey is an expensive school. He had a camel hair coat and fur-lined gloves, his mother sent him skates, his grandmother a large amount of cash. He is not bothered about the value of the fencing foils that he loses. He travels in taxis, and spends the night in an hotel as a matter of course. He goes to two nightclubs, buys drinks and doesn't bother to pick up his change in restaurants. He gives little thought to his extravagance, because his father is wealthy and squanders money too. He gives ten dollars to the nuns; when the price of a prostitute is five. (Interestingly, his argument with Maurice is a matter of principle.) Finally he even borrows his little sister's Christmas present money after he has thrown coins in the lake. This deliberate extravagance can, however, perhaps be seen as a desire to rid himself of possessions in themselves symbols of social snobbery.

Girls

Holden likes girls, even if they're not particularly lovely, as he says on p.6 with reference to Selma Turner. He enjoys girls' company – feeling quite at home in the Biltmore foyer waiting for Sally. He has Sally's photo at college. He finds something endearing about women; Mrs Morrow's leaving her case in the aisle, Jane rubbing her tear away and not minding his sweaty hands.

But once involved in a sexual situation, Holden is unsure of what is expected of him; he always stops if the girl asks him to, he kisses Sally but is repulsed by Sunny's overtures. He thinks Phoebe is too affectionate, and dislikes his double date with Stradlater. Although R. O. Bowen (see *Further reading*) says there are homosexual tones about Holden, he is upset by any non-heterosexual behaviour. He speculates about Luce and the wavy-naired piano player, and runs away from Mr Antolini. His behaviour indicates that he is non-assertive and idealistic about girls. His championship of the innocent and helpless, like Jane Gallagher and the nuns, shows a powerful romanticism. His inability to face the reality of adult love merely indicates that he is still immature. The women he can safely approach are all either considerably older, unavailable or related to him.

Religion

There are quite a few religious motifs in the book apart from Holden's resemblance to the Prodigal son, which is considerable.

He is rich, spends all his money, mixes with low, hedonistic people and returns home when he has nothing left. There is also an interesting echo of the parable of the rich man being unable to enter heaven until he has disposed of all his goods. This Holden finally does in the park.

Robert O. Bowen in 'Charity Against Whom?' thinks that Holden was an anti-Catholic, and apart from the Quaker, Arthur Childs, that seems to be the only kind of Christianity Holden encounters. He comments on Catholics preferring the company of their own persuasion; he considers joining a monastery but rejects it, and greatly admires the nuns he meets.

There are also several overt references to religion. Although he calls himself an atheist, Holden is trying to come to terms with Allie's death. He wonders about the character of Jesus; coming to the conclusion that he is forgiving and good, he wouldn't send anyone to Hell; but neither was he a fool – he must have found the disciples a burden. He knows Jesus would have agreed about the phoniness of the Christmas show. In his own intuitive way, he finds the true meaning of Christianity, and puts it into practice. He gives far more than he can afford to the nuns, he throws away all his worldly goods; he hates no one, as he says at the end of the book. Jesus-like, he moves among sinners, trying to communicate, but is not listened to or understood. Ian Ousby (see p.92) calls him a 'Holy Innocent'.

Holden substitutes the memory of Allie for religion, and casts Allie as a saint. He talks to Allie when he needs support; after the Sunny affair and when he feels he's disappearing. He often muses about Allie, and keeps an absurd memento – the baseball mitt, as a relic. Athough he knows that Allie is dead, he has not internalized the idea. He visualizes Allie lying in his grave with bunches of flowers, surrounded by dead people. Death does not frighten Holden. He thinks of it as peaceful, as attractive when he is in the museum and the park. But Salinger does not celebrate morbidity. Life always has a stronger pull.

Phoniness

Phoniness is the greatest sin in Holden's opinion. By this he implies every conceivable type of hypocrisy. He has high standards, and is rigid in their application. Actors and performers are particularly castigated for relaxing into showmen; people who behave differently to rich and poor, people who use clichés and gushing socialites are all condemned. By the time Holden has examined society very few people escape his censure – and they are either dead, like James Castle and Allie, untraceable like the nuns and Jane Gallagher, or children like Phoebe.

It can be argued that Holden often behaves hypocritically, to Mrs Morrow for instance, or making excuses to his teachers, breaking his own rules by going out with Sally, or watching the phoney film before meeting Luce. The difference is that Holden is essentially genuine. He acknowledges his faults and tries to be honest and behave equally to all.

Alienation, communication, quest and time

As Arthur Heiserman and James E. Miller point out (see p.92), Holden is a loner. His family has disintegrated after Allie's death; his mother is nervous and unsociable, his father squanders money, and D.B. is in the depth of phoniness, Hollywood. His friends are all older, so he feels left behind. He does not share society's quest for sexual dominance or materialism, because he is aware of the transience and value of life, as he makes clear to Sally at the ice-rink. Phoebe is right when she says that nothing pleases him; yet the book is not negativistic in its attitude. He sees the truth clearly; all that matters is love and its communication. But nobody wants to know. He is constantly wakening people up, Ackley, Faith, Sunny, Phoebe, and yet nobody except Phoebe listens to him. He will not compromise as all but a handful of people have done, and finally can envisage no refuge from the world except in flight.

Holden's capitulation and return with Phoebe can be seen either as the triumphant dominance of his love for his sister, or as the beginning of that compromise with the world's values which all adults have to make, and therefore a betrayal of himself. Ihab Hassan pointed out that he is at once both rebel and victim.

The quest for love is symbolized by the tantalizing figure of Jane Gallagher, and to a lesser extent by almost all the women in the book, from each of whom he seeks a different type of love. His mother has failed him, Jane is absent, and one by one all but Phoebe reject him. Jane is never accessible, enabling Holden to avoid facing reality.

The book has an air of timelessness: Holden wanders in limbo and it is disconcerting to realize that his journey lasts a mere three days. He is conscious both of time passing and of the wish to hold it back. He notes wonderingly that Phoebe is ten now, no longer a young child. He cherishes the ideal of youth, almost wishing time would stand still, as in the museum.

Films, theatre and books

Literature and the arts are a means of escape for Holden, used when life is too much to bear. He turns to a book to take his mind off Mr Spencer, and to a film after his row with Sally. He dramatizes his personal suffering by using clichés from gangster films. Some of his narrative style he has taken from his favourite authors – Ring Lardner is digressive, Scott Fitzgerald obsessed by time. Hardy's characters are naturalistic. Hemingway, whom he dislikes, deals with violence and macho values. Nor does he like the highly polished acting style of Olivier, or Ernie's scintillating playing. In art as in life, honesty is all to Holden. The books he turns to are outstanding, idiosyncratic ones – and several are tragedies; *Romeo and Juliet*, *A Farewell to Arms*, *The Great Gatsby* and *David Copperfield*. His choice tells us more about his character. The books are idealized, romantic, and satisfying to read. The characters command our sympathy.

Structure

The picaresque novel

The Catcher in the Rye can be termed a picaresque novel. It is narrated in the first person, using colloquial language and it explores society through a series of episodes. It begins at the end, in the style of *Moll Flanders*, looking back over a year in Holden's life. The structure is circular, although each episode follows a linear pattern. However, the digressions fudge this, so that the total effect is rich and complicated. This book is more concerned with character than plot, whereas most picaresque novels describe events.

The novel works through a series of rejections, none particularly shattering though all emotionally violent, which lead to the disintegration of Holden in the park, and through that to an illuminated but precarious peace, echoing the mood at the beginning of the book.

Conflict

Each of the rejections can be seen as a conflict, but they provide little suspense because there are so many of them. Holden creates conflict situations, quarrelling with his schoolfriends, his girlfriend and his teachers. He is, as Phoebe points out, going through a negativistic phase. Nobody he knows reaches his standards – so he rejects them. He is in conflict with the whole of society; he hates urban life, civilization, crowds and phoneys. He argues with taxi-drivers, waiters, Faith and Maurice. He is even at odds with himself – fascinated by sex but almost intentionally putting off Faith on the phone and paying off Sunny. He longs for the quiet of the woods, but rejects the peace of the museum; he says he can't stand the movies but depends on them for the release of emotion he can't handle.

Suspense

There are few areas of suspense in the book: all are disappointing; the understated language does not allow for histrionics, and the effect of each is prosaic. In the Sunny scene he nerves himself for action, but already regrets agreeing to her visit. In the Phoebe scene he awaits discovery by his psychic mother, but she doesn't suspect his presence, and in the park when Holden seems ready to give up he is not attracted by the idea of suicide. A certain amount of pace is given to the structure by Holden's flight. He constantly runs, from Mr Spencer, Pencey, Maurice and Mr Antolini.

Climax

The scene by the roundabout is predictable from the moment when Holden tells Phoebe he's going home. It is sentimentally satisfying: the vividly drawn picture of the roundabout is soothing. Holden's release from mental agony is euphoric: but on a deeper level, he is giving up his dream of escape, compromising with life: accepting less than the finely-honed standards he had set himself, and joining the rest of society. He betrays himself.

Dramatic irony

This operates on quite a complex level because it involves Holden looking back and judging himself, while occasionally making prescient remarks to the reader. For example, he says that he must have been stupid to have asked Sally to join him in his cabin, or he tells us that we would have liked Phoebe, or gives advice like avoiding going to the cinema. The time-setting further complicates the book; we know Holden came to no harm because he is recounting events in his past. The ending is an ironic anticlimax to his dream of a more honest society.

Style

Language

Much of the appeal of *The Catcher in the Rye* lies in its accessible, slangy language. Although the idioms may not be our own, there is no mistaking either the emotion or the meaning. Holden speaks for teenagers everywhere.

The novel has been praised for its closeness to 'fifties prep school slang. To those of us reared on American films and television, such exactitude is immaterial; in fact some expressions, because foreign to us, seem startlingly fresh. Obviously some references are dated, but a surprising number are still in currency today.

Salinger achieves the voice of Holden Caulfield by a remarkable consistency of language. Many sentences trail off vaguely, suggesting that he loses the thread of his thoughts. He generalizes wildly about people, how nobody listens to him, for example, and exaggerates a good deal – about the speed of D.B.'s Jaguar or the number of magazines advertising Pencey Prep. This gives his conversation a breathless, imprecise effect. Hell, for instance, describes both heat and cold. The word 'madman' is applied to his sister and coathangers. He refers to many people as old, regardless of age. Expletives are used with thoughtless indifference to meaning. He too is disgusted by the word on the wall – which in itself draws attention to the dilution of his own swearing. He insists he's speaking the truth as though not accustomed to being believed. Italics emphasize certain words conveying their tone or emotion. This all increases the impression of actual speech.

The various levels of diction blend, adding to the realistic effect. On one level, Holden uses teenage diction, limited vocabulary and sometimes a list of clichés where one would do. His grammar is shaky, particularly in the verb 'to lie'. This inexactitude is emphasized by his occasional attempts to correct, or his remarks on the phoney euphemisms used by the Seattle trio. At a slightly more formal level he responds to nuns and waiters. Much more self-consciously he speaks to teachers. Holden's changes in dialogue are quite marked, but fall naturally into context. Salinger shows an unerring ear for speech patterns: the voices of Horwitz and Sunny are quite unmistakable. On the whole, adults speak more formally than Holden, but his vocabulary is extensive, and he occasionally uses a surprisingly complex word. Luce is the most formal speaker in the book, followed by Holden's mother when she speaks sternly to Phoebe.

Levels of diction

Various levels of diction and attitudes operate within the book. They overlap at times, creating a perspective from which the reader can assess Holden objectively. For example, adults either ignore or mother him. The three women from Seattle refuse to take him seriously, and waiters will not serve him alcohol, but although Holden notices, he misinterprets the reasons. The conversations with taxi drivers are particularly well observed. The first one is aloof, and stonewalls all Holden's advances, even his attempts at flattery in imitating his idioms. Horwitz is impatient, only half-listening. Holden has to repeat everything. The children in the park are laconic: Phoebe is excitable, Mr Spencer pedantic. Each character has his or her own speech-rhythms.

Deeper levels are explored. Holden is unaware of Luce's phoniness although the over-polite, cultured idioms of Luce's voice are faithfully reflected. The far past is revived several times in contemplative tones. He speaks to Allie as to a child or a saint. Almost a lyrical quality is established with the mention of the ducks and the Catcher fantasy.

Although Ian Ousby (see *Further reading*) suggests that Salinger is not sufficiently detached from his hero, Salinger does indicate that we should not take Holden completely at his own valuation. The reader is made aware of the attitude of others; Ackley and Luce tell him to grow up; Sally and Phoebe comment on his language and immaturity. Waiters, taxi-drivers and Sunny are patronizing. The hatcheck girl and Mrs Morrow gently mother him. The nuns treat him with concerned, soothing calm.

Imagery and symbol

Occasionally an image recurs, like the madman, or the idea of being killed by joy as much as by pain. Some stand out from the clichés, like the comparison of Ernest Morrow to a toilet seat and the cold to a witch's teat. There is a mutilation motif; Holden favours the man in the Bible who cut himself with stones, teases Ackley by saying he is blind, and doesn't wipe off the blood until he arrives at the station.

It is as if he relishes being hurt. Another motif is that of falling. The Catcher exists to save children from falling over the cliff. James Castle died jumping from a window; Mr Antolini predicts a horrible kind of fall for Holden. These two ideas convey much of Holden's mental state.

Much greater use is made of symbol. Objects take on a symbolic value when they are treated with reverence and care beyond their value. The book is punctuated with circular objects, symbolizing completion. The roundabout, the gold ring, the record and even the hat provide Holden with comfort.

The most powerful of these objects is the roundabout, eternally travelling yet going nowhere. Its music reminds Holden of childhood, and Phoebe symbolizes that by taking his place. She grabs for the ring in spite of the possibility of falling – mentioned interestingly in conjunction with the ring symbol. Life is fraught with dangers, Holden realizes, but is essentially valuable and worth striving for. The record links Holden to Phoebe when he is still searching for her – not only does it symbolize their unity but also harmony, pleasure: they dance when they are together. He breaks it, when at his lowest ebb, but tellingly saves the pieces which she later treasures. The hat is mentioned a good deal. Holden bought it when he was being ostracized; it is an affirmation of his individuality and a source of satisfaction to him. He fiddles with it when worried by Stradlater's date with Jane, puts it on backwards in fun, and says he will use it to shoot people; wearing the hat he is warmed by it going to the station, in the taxis and on the long walk back to the hotel. After giving it, unflawed, to Phoebe, he receives it back in a touching gesture from his sister. The baseball mitt is like a holy emblem. If Allie is a saint, then the mitt is a relic.

People are symbols too – Jane is almost pure symbol, virginity, purity, the unattainable – Phoebe is an earthier, vivid, child who will grow up robustly.

Viewpoint

The action is seen entirely from the viewpoint of the first-person narrator, Holden Caulfield. He acts and comments, digresses and reminisces in a 'stream-of-consciousness' style which does not entirely blind the reader to an external assessment of his character. A streak of sentimentality has been mentioned by several critics. It is sentimental of him to keep Allie's glove, and of Phoebe to keep the shattered record. His compassion for the pimps and love of the nuns can be considered sentimental too, and indeed at the end when Phoebe is on the roundabout, Holden standing in the rain, there is a moment of embarrassing emotion. However, that is the only time that Holden admits to his deepest feelings. At other times, he transmutes emotion into physical pain, or action. Physical pain he dispels with the magic of the movies, inward hurt he soothes by a trip to a nightclub or cinema.

Frank Kermode finds Holden's preoccupation with Allie obsessive and distasteful, but it seems normal enough that a sensitive teenager should question the untimely death of a brother, and what the purpose of life might be. Philip Roth considers the book teaches a spiritual elitism – Holden is searching for someone to communicate with, and despairing of ever finding anyone; but this is one of the dilemmas of adolescence.

Although many parts of the book have their humour, Holden himself has none. The occasional flash of black humour or bathos, such as his ignominious flight from both Pencey and his parents' apartment, is directed against himself, and shows an inward bitterness.

Digressions

Holden says to Mr Antolini that he prefers digressions to the logical progression of ideas, and in *The Catcher in the Rye* he works on this principle. The digressions add depth to his biography, extend his experiences and the number of people he knows. They are also interesting in themselves. Several of them, like the digression on James Castle, are parables, giving insight into his principles and philosophy. They range in length from a casual sentence or two, like the reference to the Navajo blanket, to an entire chapter about the past (Chapter

11). Each digression has independence, and in its way is memorable. They vary in tone from the cynical references to Ossenburger who makes a living out of death, to the sunlit way in which he describes Allie waiting by the golf course.

General questions

Questions on character

1 How well does the author portray minor teenage characters in the book? Mention Sally, Ackley, Stradlater and Luce.

2 How are women portrayed in the book? Mention Mrs Antolini, the various mothers, the nuns, Sunny.

3 Write a character study of Phoebe. Does the fact that she is the only person Holden can turn to have any effect on your perception of her?

4 Which aspects of Holden's personality do you find most sympathetic, and which do you find annoying?

5 How far do you think that Holden brought his breakdown upon himself, and how much do you think was related to factors beyond his control?

Questions on themes

1 It has been said that the dominant theme of *The Catcher in the Rye* is Holden's search for love. Discuss the various types of love in the novel.

2 Discuss the theme of religion in the book. It occurs in various forms, such as the nuns, the idea of joining a monastery, the Christmas show. Why is it so often mentioned?

3 There are several recurring symbols in the book; the ducks, the red hat, the record and of course the Catcher in the Rye himself. What is the purpose of these ideas, and how are they connected or reflected elsewhere?

4 Describe the function of the museum in the novel.

5 What are the various aspects of society that Holden is in conflict with?

6 Do you consider Holden's obsession with phoneys to be extreme?

7 Although much of the book is funny, Holden lacks humour. Do you agree?

Questions on structure

1 *The Catcher in the Rye* is a picaresque novel, in which the hero has many experiences in the course of a journey. Would it make any difference, in your opinion, if the episodes with Sally and Luce or Mr Antolini had been placed in a different order?

2 The structure of the novel is circular, in that the ending is mentioned in the initial chapter. Does this have any effect on the reader's perception of Holden's experiences?

3 The novel ends without appearing to resolve Holden's conflicts. Why did Salinger not finish it off more satisfyingly?

4 The interviews with Mr Spencer and Mr Antolini are remarkably similar in several ways; one beginning and one ending the book. In what ways do they differ?

5 Do you, like Holden, enjoy digressions? What is the purpose of the astonishing number of digressions in the book? Are there some we could have done without?

Questions on language

1 What difference would it make to the book if it were written in the idiom of your area or town? Would the character of Holden be any more or less credible?

2 Do you consider that there is too much use of obscene language in the book? Why did Salinger include so much?

3 This book has been hailed as an authentic rendering of teenage American speech of the 'fifties. Do you find it very dated? Are there any areas that you find difficulty in understanding? Is it now just a historical document?

4 Some of Holden's remarks are witty: many are clichéd. Give examples of his imaginative use of simile, and his creation of expressive words. Look also for his occasional use of cliché in imaginative terms.

5 There are many instances of poor grammar throughout the book. Is there a pattern to this, or does it occur at random?

Finally

This is a book from which much can be learned. Has your reading of *The Catcher in the Rye* changed your thinking or attitudes in any way?

Guideline Notes to question 1 on character

How well does the author portray minor teenage characters in the book? Mention Sally, Ackley, Stradlater and Luce.

Characters are portrayed in various ways, by what Holden, the narrator, says about them, what they do, what they say, and what other characters say about them.

It would be most helpful to list notes on each character under these headings, to see how well each area is covered, and where Salinger puts his emphasis. Take for example Sally:

(a) What Holden says about her –

He remarks several times he doesn't like her. He comments on her loud voice, her phoniness in asking him over to trim the tree, in pretending she didn't know who was on the phone, her wanting to skate just because of the little skirts, and her enjoyment of the Christmas show which Holden found so offensive. From his comments it is clear she annoys him.

(b) What Sally actually does

She accepts his invitation to the theatre, and speaks to him on the phone when he is drunk. But she confirms all that Holden says of her; she boasts of other boys asking her out, pulls away from him in the cab, she reacts in an offensively patronizing manner to Holden's suggestions of running away, she scans the foyer at the theatre for someone else to talk to, and ignores Holden when she finds George. We see her as a vain socialite.

(c) What Sally says

Her speech is laden with clichés of a different type from Holden's. She gushes about the Lunts, and Holden says she was drooling over George, the boy she met in the foyer. She doesn't understand when Holden starts his tirade, asking him not to shout, and refusing to treat him seriously. She reacts rather like Horwitz, refusing to listen.

(d) What other characters say about her.

Apart from her photo at Pencey and Mr Antolini asking after all Holden's girlfriends, she isn't mentioned by any other character.

Now prepare similar notes on the other three characters, and the conclusions will be self-evident.

Salinger's method is clear: Holden describes each character, and then we are shown an enactment of exactly what he has said. The reader is therefore confident that Holden is telling the truth. There is no interplay between the characters. All revolve around Holden and have no life outside his consciousness. They are well drawn, but lack independent life.

Further reading

J. D. Salinger's other books: *Nine Stories, Raise High the Roofbeam, Carpenters, Seymour – An Introduction, Franny and Zooey*
Mark Twain, *Huckleberry Finn*
James Thurber, *The Secret Life of Walter Mitty*
Ann Frank, *Diary of Ann Frank*

Bibliography

Simonson, Harold P. and Hager, Philip E. *Salinger's Catcher in the Rye Clamor vs Criticism.* (D. C. Heath and Co. Lexington Mass 1963). Contains a great many articles on Salinger and *The Catcher in the Rye*
The Language of 'The Catcher in the Rye' by Donald P. Costello (American Speech XXXIV October 1959)
J. D. Salinger: Some Crazy Cliff by Arthur Heiserman and James E. Miller (Western Humanities Review, X Spring 1956)
The Salinger Syndrome. Charity Against Whom? by Robert E. Bowen (Ramparts 1 May 1962)
Kings in the Back Row by Carl F. Strauch (Wisconsin Studies in Contemporary Literature 2, Winter 1961)
Ihab H. Hassan, *Rare Quixotic Gesture* (The Western Review XXI, 1956)
Ian Ousby, *An Introduction to 50 American Novels* (Has a few pages on *The Catcher in the Rye*)
Time Magazine (September 1961) Published an article on Salinger's life and work which is worth consulting.

The Cambridge Companion to English Literature
Halliwell's Filmgoer's Companion
Pears Cyclopaedia
All furnished invaluable references.

Pan study aids Titles published in the Brodie's Notes series

Edward Albee Who's Afraid of Virginia Woolf?

W. H. Auden Selected Poetry

Jane Austen Emma Mansfield Park Northanger Abbey Persuasion
Pride and Prejudice

Anthologies of Poetry Ten Twentieth Century Poets The Poet's Tale
The Metaphysical Poets

Samuel Beckett Waiting for Godot

Arnold Bennett The Old Wives' Tale

William Blake Songs of Innocence and Experience

Robert Bolt A Man for All Seasons

Harold Brighouse Hobson's Choice

Charlotte Brontë Jane Eyre Villette

Emily Brontë Wuthering Heights

Bruce Chatwin On the Black Hill

Geoffrey Chaucer (parallel texts editions) The Franklin's Tale
The Knight's Tale The Miller's Tale The Nun's Priest's Tale
The Pardoner's Tale Prologue to the Canterbury Tales
The Wife of Bath's Tale

John Clare Selected Poetry and Prose

Gerald Cote Gregory's Girl

Wilkie Collins The Woman in White

Joseph Conrad Heart of Darkness The Nigger of the Narcissus
Youth

Daniel Defoe Journal of a Plague Year

Shelagh Delaney A Taste of Honey

Charles Dickens David Copperfield Dombey and Son
Great Expectations Hard Times Little Dorrit Oliver Twist
Our Mutual Friend

Gerald Durrell My Family and Other Animals

George Eliot Middlemarch The Mill on the Floss Silas Marner

T. S. Eliot Murder in the Cathedral Selected Poems

J. G. Farrell The Siege of Krishnapur

W. Faulkner As I Lay Dying

Henry Fielding Joseph Andrews Tom Jones

F. Scott Fitzgerald The Great Gatsby

E. M. Forster Howards End A Passage to India

E. Gaskell North and South

William Golding Lord of the Flies Rites of Passage The Spire

Oliver Goldsmith She Stoops to Conquer The Good Natured Man

Graham Greene Brighton Rock The Quiet American
The Power and the Glory The Human Factor

Willis Hall The Long and the Short and the Tall

Thomas Hardy Chosen Poems of Thomas Hardy
Far from the Madding Crowd The Mayor of Casterbridge
Return of the Native Tess of the d'Urbervilles The Trumpet-Major
The Woodlanders

L. P. Hartley The Go-Between The Shrimp and the Anemone

Joseph Heller Catch-22

Ernest Hemingway A Farewell to Arms

Susan Hill I'm the King of the Castle

Barry Hines Kes

Aldous Huxley Brave New World

Henry James Washington Square

Ben Jonson Volpone

James Joyce A Portrait of the Artist as a Young Man Dubliners

John Keats Selected Poems and Letters of John Keats

D. H. Lawrence The Rainbow Sons and Lovers

Harper Lee To Kill a Mockingbird

Laurie Lee Cider with Rosie

Thomas Mann Death in Venice Tonio Kröger

Christopher Marlowe Doctor Faustus Edward the Second

W. Somerset Maugham Of Human Bondage.

Gavin Maxwell Ring of Bright Water

Thomas Middleton The Changeling

Arthur Miller The Crucible Death of a Salesman

John Milton A Choice of Milton's Verse
Comus and Samson Agonistes Paradise Lost I, II

Bill Naughton Spring and Port Wine

R. O'Brien Z for Zachariah

Sean O'Casey Juno and the Paycock
The Shadow of a Gunman and the Plough and the Stars

George Orwell Animal Farm 1984

John Osborne Luther

Alexander Pope Selected Poetry

J. E. Priestley An Inspector Calls

J. D. Salinger The Catcher in the Rye

Siegfried Sassoon Memoirs of a Fox-Hunting Man

Peter Shaffer The Royal Hunt of the Sun

William Shakespeare Antony and Cleopatra As You Like It
Coriolanus Hamlet Henry IV (Part I) Henry IV (Part II)
Henry V Julius Caesar King Lear Love's Labour's Lost
Macbeth Measure for Measure The Merchant of Venice
A Midsummer Night's Dream Much Ado about Nothing
Othello Richard II Richard III Romeo and Juliet The Sonnets
The Taming of the Shrew The Tempest Twelfth Night
The Winter's Tale

G. B. Shaw Pygamalion Saint Joan

Richard Sheridan Plays of Sheridan: The Rivals; The Critic;
The School for Scandal

John Steinbeck The Grapes of Wrath Of Mice and Men The Pearl

Tom Stoppard Rosencrantz and Guildenstern are Dead

Jonathan Swift Gulliver's Travels

J. M. Synge The Playboy of the Western World

Dylan Thomas Under Milk Wood

Flora Thompson Lark Rise to Candleford

Anthony Trollope Barchester Towers

All Pan books are available at your local bookshop or newsagent, or can be ordered direct from the publisher. Indicate the number of copies required and fill in the form below.

Send to: **CS Department, Pan Books Ltd., P.O. Box 40, Basingstoke, Hants. RG21 2YT.**

or phone: 0256 469551 (Ansaphone), quoting title, author and Credit Card number.

Please enclose a remittance* to the value of the cover price plus: 60p for the first book plus 30p per copy for each additional book ordered to a maximum charge of £2.40 to cover postage and packing.

*Payment may be made in sterling by UK personal cheque, postal order, sterling draft or international money order, made payable to Pan Books Ltd.

Alternatively by Barclaycard/Access:

Card No.

Signature:

Applicable only in the UK and Republic of Ireland.

While every effort is made to keep prices low, it is sometimes necessary to increase prices at short notice. Pan Books reserve the right to show on covers and charge new retail prices which may differ from those advertised in the text or elsewhere.

NAME AND ADDRESS IN BLOCK LETTERS PLEASE:

....

Name———————————————————————————————

Address—————————————————————————————

———————————————————————————————

———————————————————————————————

———————————————————————————————

3/87